Elvis in the
☆ Army ☆

Elvis in the
★ Army ★

The King of Rock 'n' Roll as seen by an officer who served with him

William J. Taylor, Jr.

PRESIDIO

Trade paperback edition 1997

Published by Presidio Press
505 B San Marin Drive, Suite 300
Novato, CA 94945-1340

Library of Congress Cataloging-in-Publication Data

Taylor, William J., Jr.
    Elvis in the Army : the King of Rock 'n' Roll as seen by an officer
who served with him / William J. Taylor, Jr.
        p. cm.
    ISBN 0-89141-558-0 (hardcover)
    ISBN 0-89141-627-7 (paperback)
    1. Presley, Elvis, 1935–1977—Career in the military. 2. Rock musi-
cians—United States—Bibliography.   I. Title.
ML420.P96T43 1995
355'.0092—dc20   95-11405
    [B]   CIP

Printed in the United States of America

To

Sergeant Ira Jones

and

to the memory of

Major Jack Cochran
Sergeant First Class Robert Hodges
Sergeant Elvis A. Presley

CONTENTS

ACKNOWLEDGMENTS

To the officers, NCOs, and men of the 1st Medium Tank Battalion, 32d Armor, 3d Armored Division, U.S. Army.

To my wife, Louise, and son, Nicolaus. Each year I take away innumerable hours from our precious time together to spend in research and writing. My appreciation of their unfailing understanding and good cheer is boundless.

To Shiela Brammer, my executive secretary of more than fourteen years, who worked with me on this manuscript during her off-duty hours.

To Ira Jones, whose friendship I will always cherish and to whom I am indebted for reading the manuscript of this book with great care, checking for detail, factutal accuracy, and proper perspective.

INTRODUCTION

Not much is known about Elvis Aaron Presley's active duty military service from 24 March 1958 to 5 March 1960. His army serial number was US 53310861. He earned a sharpshooter badge for the .45 pistol and M1 rifle and a marksman badge for the M2 carbine. He received a Good Conduct Medal and a 3d Armored Division Certificate of Achievement (for faithful and efficient performance of duty). He was twenty-three years old when he was drafted as a recruit and age twenty-five when he left as a sergeant E5. The fact that he made sergeant in less than two years is worth mention because that did not happen very often in those days; promotions came slowly if at all. In 1958 our nation was still feeling the effects of the Korean War, and defense spending was being reduced.

Elvis Presley was inducted into the army when he was near the top of his singing and acting career. Recruit Presley was sent to Fort Chaffee, Arkansas, where he was given a GI haircut, his dog tags, and a uniform.

He was sent along quickly with other recruits to Fort Hood, Texas, for eight weeks of basic training. Then, Elvis went though more than eight weeks of advanced training as a tank crewman.

Everything should have been in place for the rest of his two years' service in the army. He knew that he was to be assigned to the 1st Medium Tank Battalion, 32d Armor, in Germany.

But a calamity occurred. Elvis's mother fell seriously ill. He was given campassionate leave to be at her side. She died on August 14, 1958. Within days after the funeral, he was back on duty at Fort Hood. Despite the pressures of the press coverage he shipped out on the USS *General Randall* on 22 September. The ship disembarked the King of Rock at Bremerhaven, West Germany, on 1 October. Of course, the media was out in full force. Where would Elvis Presley be assigned? What would his job be?

When Elvis and I first met, he was a twenty-three year-old private close to getting promoted to private first class. I was a twenty-five-year-old first lieutenant. The only things we had in common were that both of us had volunteered for the draft, we both had gone through basic and advanced training, and we both had landed in the same battalion of about 750 men in Germany. Like everyone else my age, I knew who Elvis was. I had heard his recordings on the radio and was aware that he was becoming the rage. To Elvis, I was just another officer in his new battalion.

We did have one other thing in common: we grew up in the 1950s. The world and America were rapidly changing. It was a decade of increasing doubts among Americans about our society. We had won a great victory at the end of World War II; the United Stated had become the world's leader, or so we thought. Then in the late 1940s through the 1950s, communism began its spread in Eastern Europe, China, Vietnam and Cuba. We did not decisively win our first war against communism in Korea, although more that 33,000 American soldiers died and over 103,000 were wounded. The Soviets developed nuclear weapons, then beat us into space with the launch of *Sputnik.* In the decade 1949–59, the U.S. foreign policy of containing communism did not seem to be succeeding. This brought on a period of self doubt. Americans wondered where we stood in the world, and the threat of nuclear holocaust loomed large.

At home, the age of television arrived during that same decade. The economy was booming and Americans were spending and consuming. From 1949 to 1959, the number of households with television sets increased from 1 to 44 million! Americans learned about "the communist threat" from Sen.

Joseph McCarthy's witch-hunt, televised for all America to see. They learned about the increasing corruption in American labor unions. Americans were crushed to find out that even the entertainment industry was tainted; a major quiz show scandal was proof of this. Our youth began to question the values of American Society (I know—I was one of them). They did not challenge the political views of the times, as young people would do in the 1960s. Rather, they began looking for their own forms of expression.

Enter rock 'n' roll with the likes of Chuck Berry, Little Richard, Buddy Holly, and Jerry Lee Lewis. America's youth had found their music. Then came Elvis with his mixture of black gospel and blues and white country music. Elvis could play it fast and play it slow, sing it loud and sing it low. His unique sound, his boyish good looks, and his new way of "moving it," skyrocketed "Elvis the pelvis" into the consciousness of America's youth. He became the personification of this new form of expression.

Elvis's gyrations and the dancing style that accompanied rock 'n' roll in general were offensive to many adults. The older generation thought and America's youth and the world were going to hell in a handbasket. Movies seemed to underscore this sentiment. In *The Wild One* in 1954, Marlon Bando, sitting astride his motorcycle in a black leather jacket, was asked, "What are you rebelling against?" The answer: "Whadaya, got?"

Mad magazine entered the stage, questioning and making fun of American culture in general. *Playboy* began publishing in 1955—oh God, naked women! The new movie star, Marilyn Monroe, epitomized the new standards of sensuous sexuality that were beginning to take hold in our society.Then came the poets and writers such as Allen Ginsberg and Jack Kerouac, openly advocating non conformity, rejecting American consumerism, and advocating a search for spiritual meaning in life.

Meanwhile, desegregation was becoming a major issue. The Supreme Court outlawed racial segregation in public schools in 1954. In 1957 Arkansas National Guard troops stood with fixed bayonets to prevent black students from entering a Little Rock high school.

This was the decade in which Elvis Presley launched his career as a singer. I asked him once whether he knew what he was doing—whether he knew the time was right for a new kind of music. His answer? "Never thought about it, Lootenet. Just doing what comes naturally." Well, Elvis "naturally" appealed to youth, not just in America, but in Europe, Australia, and across the entire world.

Elvis and I both were part of this changing American social environment. He came from a poor family. I didn't. I had a good education. He didn't. But we were heading in the same direction. For Elvis army service was just a way station on the route to fame and fortune. For me, it was a challenging profession. We were two very different people, but were destined to become friends.

This book is not a comprehensive story about Elvis's life or even a complete look at his military service. It represents a snapshot of the seven months that Elvis Presley and I served in the same battalion in Germany. This account offers a new perspective, a look at events and conversation that no one else shared with Elvis, and so the book fills in important gaps not yet reported.

This book also provides a glimpse into the total duty environment in which Elvis worked and the nature of the scout platoon and the battalion in which he served while in Germany: the army barracks life, everyday training in garrison, and the field maneuvers that occupied the vast majority of Elvis's waking hours. This book also depicts the camaraderie that developed in the early months of Elvis's service with us and the personal experiences he shared with me and others.

Priscilla Presley's *Elvis and Me* and Andreas Schroer's *Private Presley* cover Elvis Presley's private life. *Soldier Boy Elvis* by Sgt. Ira Jones, my old platoon sergeant and friend tells a great deal of Elvis at his assigned army work. *Elvis in the Army* captures other situations and events in the context of the unique relationship I shared with Elvis—the relationship between a commissions officer and a young enlisted man. For whatever reasons, Elvis singled me out—a young officer about his own age—as a person he cared about, and he frequently sought me out when he had time and when the situation was right.

My style of leadership appealed to Elvis; he told me so more than once. My rank gave me authority, but I seldom used it. I didn't believe in ordering people around. Rather, I tried to set an example that I hoped soldiers would follow because they wanted to. Elvis once said, "Lootenet, I've never heard you give an order, except in formation."

I never tried to use my rank to get anything out of Elvis and was disgusted with those officers who did. I, and the other officers of our very professional battalion, didn't consider it appropriate to ask for his autograph, to ask him to pose for photographs, or to ask that he perform. Those were things that an officer just should not do. That is why it is so rare to see a photo of Elvis with an officer of the 32d Tank Battalion.

I offered Elvis my knowledge and my friendship to the degree he sought it and I considered appropriate. In return he was always respectful not of my rank but of my feelings.

We were comrades in arms and interacted mostly on a professional basis. We were together off duty only a few times. I visited his home just once and then met only Minnie Mae Presley, Elvis's grandmother (nicknamed "Dodger" for reasons I don't know) for a few minutes. I did not know the other members of his family or the people known as the "Memphis Mafia." Elvis was not a regular visitor to my home, and he met my wife and children on only two occasions. But during those seven months together in Germany, we shared many experiences. I have reconstructed them here, with the help of our old platoon sergeant, Ira Jones. All the quotes are approximations as best I can recall them, but they carry the meanings properly.

After I left Germany, Elvis and I were never again in contact. Elvis went on to be *the* superstar of rock music. I served twenty-one more years as a professional army officer. I thought of him often and prayed for him as some of the apparent agonies of his life unfolded via the media in later years. When he died in 1977, I hoped at least one of us who served with him would write about the good years he had in the military.

Finally, two years ago, one of us did just that. Sergeant Ira Jones told part of Elvis's experience in *Soldier Boy Elvis*. It is fitting that Ira Jones told the first story about Elvis's army days. Ira was the finest NCO I ever knew in my many years in the army, and I know that Elvis felt the same respect for him.

Why write this book? Why now, thirty-six years after I last saw Elvis Presley in person? I feel that I can offer important insight into Elvis Presley and the kind of person he was. Some of the publications about Elvis's last few months in Germany refer to his use of Dexedrine tablets, his alternating fits of loneliness, his anger with the many people with whom he surrounded himself at his home in Bad Nauheim. But this was not the man I knew. I never witnessed any of these traits during the time I was with Elvis in Germany.

Over the years, I have encountered some of my 32d Tank Battalion comrades from time to time. About five years ago, I learned that my old company commander, Jack Cochran, had a terminal illness, so I decided to take the lead in searching out our old buddies and putting together a battalion reunion. Twenty-eight of us met over a two-day period. It was a very special time. The camaraderie, the bonds of renewed friendships, the reminiscences, and the war stories pulled us all back together in a strong union of shared purpose and common values. Of course, we talked a lot about our individual memories of Elvis Presley. There was not a single criticism expressed. Unanimously, we remembered a fine young man who did his job to the best of his ability and tried to stay out of the limelight.

Another reason I wanted to write this book is to set the record straight. With the exception of Ira Jones's account, other books have trivialized Elvis's performance as a soldier, down-playing the fact that he worked as one of us, in a soldier's environment, which was not exactly a picnic. One recent account even states that Elvis's unit training was somewhat of a farce. I can tell you that it wasn't. It bothers me that someone can collect a bunch of photos, put together some hearsay, then state conclusively that the 32d Tank Battalion's training and maneuvers and Elvis's role in them were anything less than serious and professional. This is a gross misjudgment. It is in-nuendo, not fact.

Elvis, along with everyone else in the battalion, worked like hell in the snow, rain, sleet, and wind of harsh German win-ters. We left our families for weeks on end to be out in maneu-ver areas or on weapons firing ranges. Our training was deadly serious; after all, we were training to kill people—So-viet soldiers—if ordered to do so by President Eisenhower, our commander in chief. When off duty most of us partied as hard as we trained. But we all knew why we were in the U.S. Army in Germany, and it wasn't for fun. Our battalion's motto was "Victory or Death." We concentrated on the victory part, never forgetting General Patton's Words: "I don't want to die for my country; I want the other son of a bitch to die for his country." The first time I quoted this Patton pronouncement to Elvis Presley, his comment was "Damn right!"

Over my seven months I spent around him, I concluded that Elvis Presley cared about his comrades in arms, that he had guts, and that he would have been a brave soldier in combat. We all wished we could have done something to prevent the sorrow of his later years. But his was a life different from ours.

Elvis wasn't there in person at our battalion reunion, but I remember having the eerie feeling that he was with us in spirit, sharing a visit with men he had known in the early days of his manhood. Strange as it seems, I had the single most vivid dream of my life that night: Elvis walked to the edge of my bed, looked down, smiled, and said quietly, "Lootenet, thanks for everything you did."

CHAPTER 1

A SNAPSHOT OF ELVIS
IN THE FIELD

It was a bright, moonlit night in the spring of 1959. Private First Class Elvis Presley and I were ready to start moving out on a two-man aggressor mission. The objective: to penetrate an "enemy" tank company perimeter, locate the company commander, and capture him. Our watches showed 1:55 A.M.

"You ready, Presley?"

The reply was a grunted "Uh-huh," accompanied by a crooked, devilish smile. He was clearly enjoying himself.

The moonlight was quickly replaced by dark clouds and heavy rain. The training area in Grafenwöhr, West Germany, was already one big mud pit and this would make it worse. But Elvis and I didn't give a damn about the weather; it would work in our favor. We had a plan that we had worked out very carefully. We had eaten some hot C rations and prepared ourselves in every detail for this operation. Our baggy field trousers were all taped up so that they wouldn't make swishing sounds when we moved. Our fatigue caps were pulled down over our heads, and camouflage grease paint was smeared all over our faces and on the backs of our hands (including the bandage on Elvis's hand, where he had scratched himself on a jeep hood a few hours before).

We started the easy part, a walk of about a mile before we hit the enemy's position. Then there would be some fairly steep climbing on wet underbrush and rocks.

"Okay, you got a compass. You lead," I said.

Elvis stopped, unbuttoned his field jacket pocket, and took a bearing with the compass's luminous dial. "Got it. Let's move a little to our right front." He started walking.

After about five hundred yards we hit an open area. I paused, got out my own compass, and took a bearing. Elvis was right on course. I walked fast but crouched over, to catch up with him. We wanted to be close enough together to use hand signals out in the open and to be within whispering distance when we were in thick woods or underbrush. And we wanted to be parallel to each other: if an enemy LP (listening post) identified one of us, we didn't want to give them the opportunity to let one of us pass and then intercept the one behind. We tried to walk on wet leaves or any other vegetation to prevent our boots from making sucking sounds in the mud.

We heard the first sound of significance about fifteen hundred yards from our point of departure. Off to our left front was the unmistakable crackle of a squad radio. Some idiot manning an LP had his volume turned up too high. We froze at the sound of the radio. It was their first mistake, and Elvis knew exactly what to do. He dropped down and crabwalked on the ground over to me. *Crabwalk* (abbreviated as "cw" in our platoon jargon) was a term coined by Ira Jones to describe walking on all fours with buttocks in the air, never letting the knees hit the ground. Knees broke twigs or hit things that made noise.

"Let's move over to the right where that big tree is at the base of the hill, okay?" Elvis whispered.

I nodded agreement, and we continued the cw. I watched to see whether Elvis was trying to penetrate past the LP we'd just located. Our plan was to bypass LPs if we could, because taking those guys as prisoners was not our mission. We wanted to get to the tank company commanding officer (CO) without alerting the entire company.

We got to the big tree, and he signaled with his arm in a forward direction, meaning "move out." I waved my arms back and forth across each other to signal "no, wait." He dropped to the ground, and I cw'd over to him. "We can't go in until we find the other LP over to our right. Then we'll know how much operating room we have." He nodded in the affirmative.

"Stay here by the tree," I said softly, then moved off slowly to the right. LPs were always placed on low ground where the sound of someone approaching could be heard most easily. On low ground, there's little wind; things tend to be quiet. There had to be another LP over to the right. I crept along for twenty-five to thirty yards, hearing nothing but the rain and, now, some thunder. I stopped to catch my breath—and listened. It paid off—I heard the click of a lighter closing. A poorly trained or undisciplined soldier on an LP had lit a cigarette, a major violation of training rules. He probably was trying to hide the cigarette under a poncho, but I saw a faint glow while he puffed to get a good light.

We had marked our point of entry into the enemy's defense perimeter. I cw'd back over to the big tree and lay down next to Elvis.

"I found the next LP," pointing to our right, "about twenty-five yards away, near that outcropping of rock."

Elvis smiled and whispered, "Okay, learned somethin'."

I smiled back. "Hodges taught me." Sergeant Robert Hodges was one of the best reconnaissance NCOs (noncommissioned officer) in the army. He had taught me one hell of a lot about recon techniques.

I slapped the brim of Elvis's soaking-wet fatigue cap. "Let's go straight up, okay?"

He gave me an O with the forefinger and thumb of his hand.

I whispered, "I have the lead now, okay?" A nod in return. "Look, when we get inside that perimeter, we may find the CO's headquarters. He will have infantry with him. His command post probably will be inside an armored personnel carrier with a canvas shelter erected straight off the back. Understand?"

"Got it."

We began the climb. We were not scaling a sheer cliff, but the slope must have been about 70 percent. In the pouring rain and mud, we could easily slip and make noise, so we proceeded very slowly. We had only about forty to fifty yards to climb, but it was exhausting, even though we were both in top physical condition. (Elvis told me later that he was "dog-tired" several times during that climb and thought I'd never slow down for a breather. I admitted that I was tired too but had kept moving because I didn't want him to think I couldn't hack it. We laughed our tails off about that one! Another insight into leadership.)

We continued climbing, maybe six to eight yards apart, grabbing small tree trunks, branches, rocks—anything that would give us leverage—going up and up. We had to stop every so often, not only to rest our muscles but to listen. The scout platoon was called "the eyes and ears" of the battalion. That was more than a cliché. Our main reason for existence was not to destroy the enemy, but to find the enemy's position and report it to the battalion, which had the firepower to attack.

I had just stopped. Elvis, eyes fixed on my every move, stopped also. We tried to listen through the rain and the thunder, which was getting more frequent and louder. Both of these acts of nature worked in favor of our movement. Lightning, however, was not in our favor, and a bolt had just lit up the sky. After a minute or so, the thunder and lightning slackened, and there was nothing but the rain. We lay there listening. Again, it paid off, this time with a clank. It sounded like a hatch closing; probably one of the tank crew had closed his hatch to stop the rain from coming in. We knew that sound had to come from a tank or an armored personnel carrier (APC). And the sound told me that the vehicle was right above us and pretty damn close—maybe fifteen yards away. We had hit another major flaw in that tank company's security.

I cw'd over to Elvis. Rain was dripping down the bill of his fatigue cap.

"How's your hand?" I asked.

"Nuthin', Lootenet."

"Okay. Let's go up and eyeball them."

He nodded and we moved ahead. Suddenly we were at the top of the ledge, staring into two tank treads and the bottom of the front deck of an M48 medium tank (fifty tons worth). As I looked straight up, I could see the barrel of a 90mm main gun. Our next obstacle.

I had done this type of aggressor duty many times before, but it was new to Elvis. He cw'd over toward me very slowly. "Now what? Take the tank?"

"Let's wait and listen some more," I whispered. He nodded.

After maybe five minutes Elvis turned to me. "Shit, we can go up right past 'em."

He sensed that the tank crew had let their guard down. They were loafing on the job.

"Lead the way," I said.

He motioned me to the right of the tank and moved to the left himself. We inched along the tank treads, moving very slowly. Another big flash of lightning, and we both dropped to the ground. My face went into a mud puddle made by the tread. I spat out the dank mud, feeling the grit between my teeth. For a couple of minutes I couldn't see anything because the lightning had destroyed my night vision. Then I felt a movement on my left side. It was Elvis.

"Let's move," I said.

We cw'd maybe twenty more yards beyond the tank, moving pretty fast now because the thunder was loud and would drown out any sound we would make.

The lightning and thunder struck again, a pretty long roll and a flash as bright as daylight. And there, just ahead of us, was an APC with the telltale canvas shelter erected behind it— our target. This method of setting up a command post (CP) was convenient because the shelter provided expanded working space, but I had always thought it was a bad idea. The shelter tied down the CP, taking away its capability to move immediately, and it also made it easy for an infiltrator to identify where a unit commander most likely would be located. Right now, Elvis and I were about to take advantage of what we saw.

A lone guard armed with an M3 "grease gun" (a small, stubby .45-caliber machine gun) was standing behind the CP.

"Ten meters to go," I whispered. "I'll just walk up to him, hand him a tag, tell him he's a POW, and we'll walk in."

Elvis grinned. "Let me get that guy. If he makes trouble, I'll give him a round kick."

Elvis is really getting into karate, I thought.

"Come on," I replied, "no bullshit."

Elvis asked softly, "Okay. But how's about I get him, and you walk in and grab the CO?"

Private First Class Presley wanted to do his thing. I nodded, then crouched and got ready to move. Elvis stood up, looking like a walking mud pile, and walked over to the CP guard. "Your ass is mine," he said, much too loudly, sticking his empty grease gun close to the guy's nose.

I ran fast through the back of the canvas shelter, up the lowered back ramp of the APC, yelling, "Aggressor here. You're captured!"

Three people—a captain, a first lieutenant, and a master sergeant—were working at a plastic-covered map taped to one of the steel walls of the APC. The captain looked stunned. So did the lieutenant. The sergeant looked resigned and said quietly, "Oh, shit."

I dug into my pockets for the buff-colored POW tags and handed one to each of them. "Please tie these onto the straps of your web gear."

The lieutenant made a face I didn't much like, so I asked him to step aside, and I moved to the radio. I switched it to the umpire channel, picked up the microphone, keyed it, and said, "Yellow Ribbon Three, this is Champion Two-Six. Have captured Rocket Six. Coordinates follow."

"Presley, bring in your prisoner," I called out.

Elvis walked in behind a bedraggled private wearing a steel helmet and poncho.

"We got 'em all, Lootenet?"

I nodded in the affirmative. "How about checking the map and giving me the eight-digit coordinate of where we are."

Elvis studied the map, then pointed to a place and read off the coordinates. I repeated them into the hand mike, then released the transmit switch.

The reply came back: "Rocket Six, this is Yellow Ribbon Three. Confirm capture."

The company commander looked at me with a dejected expression. He depressed the mike and said, "This is Rocket Six. Capture confirmed."

All six of us stood there, bent over in the low-topped APC, looking awkwardly at one another. At that tense moment, it was Elvis who spoke up.

Looking directly at the short, stocky company commander, Elvis said, "Sorry, Sir."

The captain stared at Elvis for a moment, then turned to me. "Either you guys are good, or my security needs a lot of beefing up. Well, either way, we'll all learn something from this."

There were some arrogant officers in the army in those days, but that captain obviously was not one of them. He took a couple of steps toward us and clapped us both on the shoulder. "Fine job. Who are you? What are your ranks?"

We had put brown tape over our name tags and rank insignia. In those days name tags were white, the PFC insignia was green and yellow, and the first lieutenant insignia was white. They could be seen in the dark, so had to be covered up. "Lieutenant Taylor, Sir."

"Private First Class Presley, Sir."

The lieutenant said with a quizzical look, "Are you *the* Elvis Presley?" Oh, boy, I thought, what a jerk this guy is. We all ignored him.

"Captain," I said, "the only thing that counts is that we are with an aggressor force, part of which is still out there in the rain. Let's check with umpire control and see whether we can call off this operation."

"Affirmative. Wait."

The captain keyed the APC radio and asked whether the exercise was completed. I could hear the affirmative reply. It was about 3:45 A.M. I asked the captain to have his tank crews turn on their lights and flash them to signal that the exercise was over. Sergeant Jones and the others would then walk on into the perimeter. The captain radioed his platoon leaders and gave the order.

Elvis and I stepped outside the canvas cover over the back of the APC and could see vehicle lights and flashlights all over the place. The captain stepped out also and asked the APC commander, a sergeant, to heat up some water for coffee. Within a few minutes two little stoves had done the job, and the APC crew produced aluminum packets of instant coffee. Elvis and I weren't wearing our web belts, so we didn't have our aluminum canteens and cups. The APC crew gave us their cups, and we sipped hot coffee.

A few minutes later I noticed the lieutenant was talking with Elvis over by a big tree. Elvis looked very uncomfortable; he kept looking down and shuffling his feet. Then I saw that the lieutenant had a notebook and pen in his hand and was holding it out to Elvis—who wasn't taking it. I walked over to them.

"Hey friend," I said to the lieutenant, "let's talk a minute over there by the APC." As the man turned to look at me, Elvis rolled his eyes, then shook his head rapidly in a "yes, Lord, yes" affirmative.

The lieutenant protested. "Hey, I'm busy," he whined. Right then, Elvis made a quick escape.

"What in hell were you doing?" I asked the lieutenant.

"None of your business" was his reply.

"Don't you have any common sense, you jerk? Leave Presley alone. He's doing his job."

The man stepped forward, put his face right up to mine, and slowly said, "Go mind your own fucking business!"

That did it. I gave him a hard, straight shot right in that tender little spot just below the chest cavity. He went down, doubled up and gasping for air. I left him there, walked the few meters over to the APC, and began chatting with the captain. I hoped like hell that no one had seen me hit the guy.

Before long Sgt. Ira Jones and the others started ambling up to the APC looking like muddy, drowned rats. Other cups of coffee were produced, and we stood around shooting the breeze about the operation. At about 5:30 A.M., we could see BMNT (beginning of morning nautical twilight). The captain walked over to tell us that he had called for a two-and-a-half-ton truck to come pick us up so that we wouldn't have to walk the mile or so back to the recon platoon area. He really was a good man, and I felt rather sorry that we had ruined his exercise. He would be graded as a failure on night security by the umpire team, and that would mean a black mark on the company's training record. I had the idea that somehow he would make corrections in his company training and that this episode would accomplish its purpose—getting another army unit ready to fight a war with the Soviets, a war we all hoped like hell would never happen.

The truck rolled in, and I saluted the captain. So did Sergeant Jones, Elvis, and the others.

He returned the salute with a smile. "You guys are one hell of a fine team. Keep it up."

The lieutenant was nowhere to be seen as we boarded the back of the truck and took off for the platoon area.

All of us were exhausted. When we dismounted near our jeeps, Jones ambled over to Elvis, put an arm around his shoulder, and said, "Good job. All of you guys did it right."

I walked over to Elvis and slapped him on the shoulder.

"Lootenet, I saw. Damn, you got him pretty good. What an asshole. Feel good?"

"Well, there aren't many officers like that guy in our army, thank God."

"Maybe not in the battalion, but let me tell you, there are plenty of them around. You should have been at Chaffee."

"Do you really have to put up with much stuff like that?"

"Not when Sergeant Jones, Lootenet Hart, or Colonel Williams know about it, but sometimes a guy like that lootenet tries to pull an end around. And, *for sure* not when you're around," Elvis said with a big, broad smile.

What a position to be in! If Elvis had decked the lieutenant himself, the guy could have brought charges against him. A no-win situation for sure. In fact, the lieutenant could have brought charges against me, but I knew he wouldn't.

"The guy was pushing for your autograph, right?"

"Uh-huh."

"Why not just sign the damn thing and get it over with?"

"Well, Lootenet, that's my choice, and I didn't like the guy's attitude or the things he said."

"I see. Well, it's over."

"Yeah. But thanks. Thanks for the whole night. I'll remember this one as kinda' special."

Me too, I thought to myself. "See you later." No salutes were necessary.

CHAPTER 2

ELVIS ARRIVES

lvis Presley arrived at the port of Bremerhaven, West
Germany, on 1 October 1958. He got lucky in his assignment. He could have been sent to any army unit
anywhere in the world, but he was assigned to a tank
battalion in Friedberg, about twenty miles north of Frankfurt.
The 1st Medium Tank Battalion, 32d Armor, 3d Armored Division—known to most GIs as the 32d Tank Battalion—was one
of the best battalions in the U.S. Army. Our motto was "Victory
or Death." We always joked that the alternatives stated in the
motto gave us no real choice but to be good enough to win.

A tank battalion in those days had about 750 men and seventy-two tanks divided into five companies. The headquarters
and service company generally supported the rest of the battalion with vehicle and radio maintenance, supplies, and administration, but it also had three small combat-type units.
One was a newly reorganized scout platoon. When I had commanded that platoon, it was called a reconnaissance platoon
and was armed with two light tanks, two personnel carriers,
and six jeeps. The scout platoon now had only jeeps, a few of

which mounted .30-caliber machine guns. There was also a mortar platoon armed with 4.2-inch mortars (the battalion's own close-in artillery support) and a tank section of four medium tanks, one for each of the four most senior officers in the battalion. There were four tank companies, A through D, each with about 120 men and seventeen tanks. The tank companies were the main combat maneuver units—the muscle and guts behind the battalion's awesome firepower, mobility, and shock action. Eventually, the scout platoon became Elvis's military home.

Most of our company commanders and senior NCOs were experienced soldiers, hardened from combat in World War II and the Korean War. They were determined that their men would never go into combat unprepared. Most were solid leaders who knew how to get the best out of their subordinates by setting an example, by knowing their stuff about tanks and armored warfare, by teaching their men well and training them hard, and by being consistently loyal to their men.

When Elvis arrived in the 32d Tank Battalion, I had recently been promoted to executive officer of B Company, after one and a half years of commanding the recon (later scout) platoon to which he would be assigned. I had mixed feelings about that promotion because it was hard to leave the recon team that Sgt. Ira Jones and I had built together and loved so much. Jones and I were fiercely proud of every man in the platoon and knew that the feeling was mutual. Neither of us could hold back tears at my final formation with the platoon on 9 November 1957. I knew I would keep tabs on what the platoon was doing. It would be hard to stay away for many reasons, including the fact that B Company and the platoon lived and worked so closely together.

Most of us in the 32d didn't know that Elvis would be assigned to our battalion until we heard about a press conference held at 3d Armored Division headquarters in Frankfurt. It was interesting news, but we didn't have a hell of a lot of time to think about it. We were working our tails off getting ready to move the whole battalion from our *Kaserne* (the German word for base) at Ray Barracks near the small town of Friedberg, to a big tank training area for gunnery practice. The training area at Grafenwöhr, West Germany, was about 110 miles to the east near the Czechoslovakian border, which separated the free west from the communist east. All our track and wheel vehicles were old, and we were trying to get them in the best shape possible.

Elvis initially was assigned to D Company, a very good company which, unfortunately, was having leadership problems. The company commander, Captain Russell, had recently taken over from Capt. Ed Beckner, one of the best company commanders in the battalion. It's difficult for any new commander to take over from a great leader, and Russell was in just such an awkward situation. I had heard from friends that Russell was not relating well to his NCOs.

On the morning after Elvis joined D Company (the first week in October 1958), we heard through the grapevine that he had been assigned as Russell's jeep driver. I thought at the time that this was a mistake. A celebrity like Elvis reporting to a new unit should have been assigned to a tank crew to become (as much as possible) a regular member of a combat team, instead of being stuck out there like a sore thumb as the CO's jeep driver. It could only have made him more self-conscious.

During the first few days, all kinds of rumors floated around the battalion area: reporters were trying to get past the military police gate guards to get interviews with and photos of Elvis. Telephones in battalion headquarters and D Company were ringing off the hooks. Tons of mail and packages were arriving in the mailbags for Elvis. German girls were trying to crawl over or under the Kaserne fences just to get a glimpse of the superstar. There was a lot of confusion going on in the D Company area.

After only a few days, I received a telephone call from the battalion's sergeant major, Ed Hackney.

"Hey Sir, the Old Man wants to talk with you. We got a problem." It was an army custom to call the person in command, whether a colonel or a lieutenant, "the Old Man."

I told him I would be right over and quickly walked the couple hundred yards from B Company to battalion headquarters. I hoped that the problem didn't have anything to do with my company.

To get to battalion headquarters, I had to pass by the recon platoon barracks. As always, a wave of nostalgia came over me as I looked at the big yellow sign on the corner. It was the platoon's insignia, which we had designed ourselves, then paid a local German shop to paint shortly after I took command of the platoon. On the sign was a caricature of a wild wolf in a recon jeep going full speed, cross-country. We also had a tailor shop make patches of the recon insignia to be sewn on a shoulder loop that could be slipped over the sleeve of our army field jackets and held in place by the shoulder epaulet. These were given to all the platoon members. It was against regulations to wear such patches, but I knew it would be great for morale. The platoon was damn good, and we all knew it. We were the only recon platoon in the battalion; we were different and thrived on the distinction. Elvis Presley was to wear his patch with great pride after he became a team member.

I entered the battalion headquarters building and walked into the office of Sergeant Major Hackney and the S1 (the battalion adjutant). Hackney, the ranking sergeant in the entire battalion, was the kind of old professional NCO who ate lieutenants for breakfast. He was tough as nails and nobody—I mean nobody—messed around with him.

"Go on in, the Old Man's waitin' for ya'." Hackney clicked his false teeth together for emphasis—a crazy habit of his.

I walked past Hackney's desk into the office of Lieutenant Colonel Williams, who sat at his desk with an American flag and a 32d Tank Battalion flag on either side of his chair. The 32d flag had a large number of streamers attached to the top, just under a large brass spearhead. Each streamer had sewn on

it the name of a famous battle that the battalion had won in
wars over its long history. Williams was a tall, slender guy,
semibald and graying, with a southern drawl. He was a fine
commander, liked and respected by all of us .

"Bill, I need your advice. We've got problems about Private
Presley. All the reporters, phone calls, and that kind of stuff are
driving Captain Russell crazy."

Williams stood up and looked out his window. He could
see both the scout platoon and the D Company barracks
across the street.

"I mean, really, Russell may have a nervous breakdown. He
just can't seem to deal with this situation."

Williams paused, turned around, and put both hands on the
back of his desk chair. "What do you think about moving
Presley out of D Company and into the scout platoon? You
know that platoon better than anyone else."

What a great idea, I thought. Colonel Williams was one
smart dude. The new scout platoon leader, Lt. Ed Hart, was a
good man. He was a hands-off leader (unlike me), but he del-
egated a lot of authority to his platoon sergeant, Ira Jones.
Jones was a six-foot-four, tough (like a velvet hammer), self-
confident, patient old combat veteran who loved to play the
"good ol' country boy" routine. Yes, Jones was a pro. He had
started his service in the Arkansas National Guard before
World War II, participated in Operation Overlord (the Normandy Beach landing under General Eisenhower), fought as
an infantry NCO across France and Belgium, won the Silver
Star for bravery under German artillery and mortar fire, and
was wounded and awarded the Purple Heart—he had learned
professional soldiering the hard way. His preoccupation in life
was to teach everything he knew to his soldiers and to his officers. I had been his platoon commander and his student simultaneously. I had been lucky to serve so closely with him,
and Elvis would be lucky to be assigned to his platoon. Jones
was a father figure to all the young men in the platoon; Elvis
would be fortunate to have someone like Ira Jones around him

at that juncture in his life. And Hart and Jones would be able to handle the reporters and all the notoriety while shielding Presley and giving him the kind of training every good soldier wanted and deserved.

"That's one hell of a good idea, Sir." Colonel Williams asked me why, and I told him what I thought. He smiled. He obviously had already figured out the situation and was just bouncing his pending decision off me for good measure. "Okay, Bill, thanks."

He had never called me by my first name before this meeting. I snapped to attention, saluted, and walked out past Sergeant Hackney, who was working on a pile of papers on his desk. He never looked up as he snapped his false teeth together.

"See you, Sir. I knew you'd agree. Jones can handle Presley," said Hackney.

Ira Jones told me later that he got the word that same day. The next day Elvis moved his gear directly across the main battalion road into the scout platoon's two-story, masonry barracks building.

A rumor immediately started running around about the reason for Elvis's transfer out of D Company. The story was that he had a little-known ear problem and couldn't be around loud noises. Lord knows you can't find many noises louder than the horrendous crack-boom of a 90mm main gun on a tank. That rumor didn't make much sense to me, however. It's implausible that the army medical exam system had failed to detect such an ear problem long before Elvis was assigned to a tank company. In any case, I knew the real reason he was taken out of D Company—the reason Colonel Williams had shared with me.

That evening, I drove the fifteen to twenty minutes or so home from the Kaserne to the apartment housing area where married lieutenants and sergeants lived with their families. The area was called "Little Texas" for some reason I never did figure out. When I parked our 1952 Ford and walked up the stairwell to our second-floor apartment, my two little children, Jill and Tod, were already at the door to provide the hugs and kisses that meant so much to me. My wife, Peggy, pregnant with our third child, was cooking dinner. She smiled and gave me a kiss. It wasn't every day that I could get home by six o'clock for dinner with my family. And often I was gone for weeks at a time for field training with the rest of the battalion.

Peggy "uncorked" a German beer for me—the local beer came in bottles with ceramic stoppers and rubber seals held in place by wires. She asked me about my day, and I told her about Elvis Presley. I told her that Presley probably was going to be reassigned to the scout platoon.

She gave me a glance, the same one she gave me every time I mentioned the platoon. "You still love that darn platoon, don't you?"

She was fascinated by the news about Elvis Presley. Obviously, she listened to the radio a heck of a lot more than I did (military families didn't have televisions in Germany) and was more aware of the changes going on in popular music and the rise of new rock stars.

Peggy asked a few questions about Elvis, but I couldn't begin to answer them. I didn't know where he had taken basic training. Hell, until a few days ago, I wasn't even aware that he had entered the army.

The next morning I met Elvis Presley for the first time. I had just stopped by the motor pool to see my old recon jeep driver Pfc. Virgil Box, who was pulling maintenance on my old jeep, HQ26 (with the nickname "Hustler" stenciled on the side). Elvis was driving Sgt. Ira Jones in a jeep, and I ran into them as I walked around a corner. Jones asked him to stop, uncoiled his lanky frame from the front seat, and saluted me in his typical, easygoing way.

"Sir, I want you to meet the newest member of our platoon." Jones and I walked around the front of the jeep as Elvis turned off the engine, dismounted, came to attention, and saluted.

"Mornin', Lootenet," he said with a smile. I had never seen an Elvis Presley smile (I had never even seen one of his movies). Although a bit crooked, his smile was genuine and captivating. "Heard about you, Lootenet."

I returned his salute and held out my hand. He had a good handshake—real firm—and he looked me right in the eyes. That was a good start. We were roughly the same height, a little over six feet, and the same build. He had a good military bearing and "presence." I liked him right away. I noted that he wore a ring on each of his little fingers, gold with little black stones of some kind. I wondered how he could pull maintenance with rings on.

I noticed too that he was wearing well-shined tanker boots. That was easy to notice because darn few people could afford to own a pair. The army issued plain black leather boots, which were functional but not very attractive. They had soft toes and did not keep a spit shine very well because when the leather bent, the spit shine cracked and looked lousy. So, many of us, especially officers, spent some extra money to buy jump boots (like paratroopers wore) at the post exchange (PX). At about twenty-eight dollars a pair in those days, they were considered expensive, but they had hard toes supported by a metal insert. The leather on the toe did not bend, and they kept a brilliant spit shine. Tanker boots were about forty-five dollars a pair and had to be special ordered. But Elvis Presley had on a pair, and they glistened. I learned later that Elvis competed in boot shining with everyone in the platoon—and usually won.

Elvis wore his fatigue uniform well. It was clean, neat, and starched—just right. Like the spit shine, a heavily starched uniform was part of "the army way" in the 1950s. And Elvis's fatigue cap was properly blocked. (Another army tradition that didn't make much sense. After all, the purpose of a fatigue cap was to wear it for work, then crumple it up and put it in your pocket when necessary).

"Presley, you are the luckiest guy in the world to be in the recon platoon," I told him.

"Uh, *scout* platoon," corrected Jones.

"Already know it, Lootenet." "Lootenet" (with a long "loo") was all he called me from then on (except once) in the following months that we served together in the 32d Tank Battalion.

Elvis and I met again later that same day. That afternoon my wife, two kids, and I picked up her parents at the Frankfurt Airport and drove them to the Park Hotel, an elegant establishment in Bad Nauheim. We agreed to meet them back at the hotel at 6:30 P.M. for drinks and dinner. We went back to our apartment to change, then left at six o'clock to go back to the Park Hotel. I dropped Peggy at the entrance, parked our car, and hurried in—and there in the lobby were Sergeant Jones and Elvis, both wearing fatigue uniforms.

"Hey guys, what are you doing here?"

Elvis looked tired but smiled and tugged at his fatigue cap.

"Well, Sir, Elvis has some family and friends checkin' outta' here. They're all movin' to another place. I'll fill ya' in later."

That confused me, but I was in a hurry. "Okay, see you later."

I took the elevator up in the company of an Arab wearing the traditional robe and a *Kaffiyeh*, the headcloth held on by a gold embroidered headband. I thought they might be members of a royal family from some Middle Eastern country. Later, I found out that I was right—they were from the Saudi royal family. I also found out that that was why Elvis and his family had decided to move to another hotel—the royal family was attracting media attention to the hotel.

When I told Peggy and her parents what Jones had said, she was as puzzled as I. Unmarried soldiers had to live on the base, or so we thought. It had never crossed my mind that dependents could be other than wife and children, and that, therefore, a soldier could be entitled to live off post with them. But Elvis was a special case in more ways than one.

We had an elegant but short dinner at the Park. Peggy's parents were tired and jet-lagged from what in those days was a long and circuitous flight from New York to Frankfurt. As we walked out of the dining room through the lobby, I saw Jones and Presley again. I asked Peggy and her parents to go up to their suite, saying I would come up shortly.

Jones and Presley both stood as I walked over to them. "You still here?"

Jones looked a bit irritated, and Presley appeared even more tired than before.

"Well," Ira Jones began most statements with "Wel,l" "Sir, it's takin' 'em a long time to get all their stuff ready."

I thought a second and asked, "Why don't we have a beer? I have a little time if you want. My wife's upstairs with her parents. Presley, why don't you just ring up your family and tell them you'll be in the dining room until they're ready to go?"

Elvis looked at Ira Jones and they nodded to each other, then to me. Elvis walked to the front desk and spoke on the house phone. "All set," he said when he returned.

We walked to the hotel's dining room with me in the lead. I went right to the tuxedoed headwaiter to make sure it would be okay to have two soldiers in fatigue uniform with me in a rather formal dining room. As he looked over my shoulder, he assured me that he knew who Elvis Presley was and that everything would be just fine. He led us to a table in a corner. I asked Jones and Presley to order first. Jones ordered a local beer, Elvis a Coke, and I a Rhine wine.

When our drinks had been delivered, I raised my glass and toasted to victory or death. As we all took a drink, I noticed a quizzical look on Presley's face.

"To *what*, Lootenet?"

I looked from Presley to Jones, saying, "Well, Master Sergeant Jones, I see that the socialization process is a little slow nowadays."

Jones replied, "Kinda' been busy the last few days." He then explained to Presley that "Victory or Death" was the motto of the 32d Tank Battalion and that we did not know for sure where the motto came from, but it meant we were focused on beating the Soviets if they dared to attack and would die in battle before ever surrendering even one man.

Elvis Presley just stared at Jones for a few seconds. So did I as I reflected one more time on the facts that those of us in the U.S. Army were in quite a different business from our friends back home, and that we had better know our business cold. I thought also that Elvis Presley was new to our business and would need a lot of leadership and training to make him as competent as the other members of the scout platoon he had just joined.

Jones got up and excused himself. "Got to call my wife and let her know where I am. Be right back."

"Heard you'll soon make private first class. Congratulations," I said to Presley.

"Kinda' automatic," he replied, looking down at his Coke pensively.

"You're going to have a great tour over here. Lieutenant Hart and Sergeant Jones are real professionals. You have some great NCOs in your platoon, some of the very best. The guys are great at their jobs. They'd better be, because I trained a lot of them."

"Like I told you, Lootenet, one of the guys pointed you out on the main road the other day and told me who you are. You outta be proud."

"I am proud of everyone in the platoon and glad that you're in it. That platoon was my first real command in the army. It was the command I wanted but never really thought I'd get, for many reasons. I really got lucky."

"Lootenet, I think you make your own luck in life. I've been lucky, but no Lady Luck gave it to me. I had to work hard to make luck. Don't believe stuff happens by chance. The Lord doesn't let things happen by chance."

Elvis had his head in his hands, elbows on the table, thinking out loud. Boy, did he look tired.

"Well, when I say luck, I mean somethin' more, a lot more. I really mean that the Lord looks after me. I grew up in the

Episcopal Church and went for nine years to a school called Episcopal Academy in Philadelphia. I learned that I'm in the hands of the Lord, but the Lord expects me to bust my tail to do the right thing accordin' to his rules."

At that point, Ira Jones ambled to the table. "We got about five more minutes they say, then we're on our way. The cars are still waitin' outside."

Jones looked squarely at me and rolled his eyes upward. He dropped his big frame heavily into his chair, exhaled deeply, and took a long swig of his beer. "Everything's okay, no problem," he said, looking first at Presley, then me.

I knew that Sergeant Jones was dealing with a pain-in-the-ass situation, but I also knew that he was in charge—whether or not the other people involved knew it. I thought to myself that if Private Presley watched Jones over the next few months, he would learn a hell of a lot about "taking charge" (or leadership). That big-ass, relaxed, Arkansas-born master sergeant could put people and resources together in a way that made good things happen. And he did it in a way that made his men think that it was their idea, not his.

I took a fast glance at my watch. It was almost 8:45 P.M. Although I knew that Peggy and her parents had lots to talk about, I realized that her parents were very tired. We had to get our baby-sitter home, and I had to get up at 4:30 A.M. the next morning.

An assistant hotel manager walked up to our table to announce in a thick, gutteral German accent that "the Presley party" was ready to depart. We didn't waste any time getting up. All three of us were ready to go.

The next words we exchanged were important because they proved to be the essence of the Presley-Jones-Taylor relationship for the next seven months.

Sergeant Ira Jones said: "Well, we got some interestin' times ahead of us. Gonna be okay. Gonna be fun. Gonna be hard sometimes, but old recon is gonna win every time. Right, Sir?"

Elvis waited, I guess to see if I was going to say anything. Then he seemed to put his fatigue behind him. "I feel pretty good about all this," he said to us. "Feel really good about bein' with this outfit. People are different here. Know what you're doin'. I'm gonna do my job, hope you know that. People who care, count. Thanks."

Delighted to hear words like that from any soldier new to our battalion, I replied, "I'll be around for another seven months or so. If you need me, call on me."

Ira Jones started to walk out. "Let's get this show on the road."

At that moment a guy from Presley's entourage walked into the dining room, saying, "We're ready. Let's go?"

"See you later," I said, as I walked to the lobby to call Peggy on the house phone.

As we drove back to our apartment housing area in Little Texas, Peggy wondered out loud whether having Presley, his entourage, and the media around would cause changes in the 32d. I wondered too. We were a tightly knit outfit of soldiers who trained and played hard. It sounds insensitive to say so, but our mission came first, and our family life just had to fit in whenever possible. We also didn't have much time for outsiders. Although my first encounters with Elvis Presley impressed me, I still wondered whether The King of Rock 'n' Roll would really fit in. If not, we were all going to have trouble.

CHAPTER 3

GETTING ELVIS INTEGRATED

The next day I was up at 4:30 A.M. as usual, arriving in the B Company area a little before six, in time for reveille and the morning run. Later in the morning, I walked over to the scout platoon barracks and found the entry door propped open. I looked in to the left and saw Sgt. John Callender, one of the scout section leaders (there were two sections of four machine-gun jeeps each), giving a class on reconnaissance techniques. Callender was a sharp-looking, chunky guy with a close crew cut—maybe in his late twenties.

I didn't want to walk into the barracks area because it was army custom for enlisted men to stand at attention when an officer entered the room. Why break up a class? Everyone was listening carefully to Callender, who had thoroughly studied recon techniques and taught with great care and rigor. He asked a lot of questions as he taught, and no one wanted to give the wrong answer and get hazed by other members of the platoon.

There sat Pvt. Elvis Presley with a notepad and pencil, paying very close attention to what Callender was saying.

"So, when you're not sure where you are on the map, always go another mile or two in the same direction before you turn back. Most often, you ain't gone far enough."

Callender paused, looked up, and saw me in the back of the room. He grinned. "Lieutenant Taylor, he knows. Right?"

"At ease," I said immediately, so that no one would call the group to attention.

The guys turned around, looked a little surprised, and smiled. A few of them waved (most unmilitarily).

Callender was ending up his map-reading class, and he used a line from his predecessor, Sgt. Bob Hodges, a legend in the recon platoon: "Any recon guy who tells you he's never been lost is lying through his teeth. Okay, take fifteen."

Everyone got up and stretched. Most ambled outside for a smoke break. Callender caught Elvis's eye and motioned for him to come over to where we were.

"Hey, Sir, you met Elvis?"

"Yes, Sergeant, Private Presley and I have met," I replied.

Callender yawned deeply and said, "Okay, light 'em up," taking a fat cigar out of his pocket.

Sergeant Ira Jones ambled up next to me, took out a pack of cigarettes, shook one out, and held the pack out to me.

When I declined, Callender looked at me skeptically. "Oh shit, Lieutenant, how long this time?"

I had quit smoking for almost three months at that point.

Elvis didn't smoke then either. Later, I did see him light up once in a while, and he loved to chew on cigarillos.

We all walked out into a bright, warm sun. Callender looked across the street toward D Company, then walked over to talk to someone he knew.

Elvis looked down at a scuff on the right toe of his spit-shined boots, crossed the boot behind his left leg, and rubbed it lightly on his fatigue trousers.

"Where you from, Lootenet?"

I told him that I had lived most of my life outside Philadelphia.

"Saw you downtown with your wife and kids. Good lookin' family. Looks like you're gonna have another one."

It flashed through my brain that our battalion was due for field training at "Graf" right when our baby was to be born. Damn. I hadn't been around when our second baby, Tod, was born; now it looked like it might happen again. Army life surely wasn't easy on the family.

I asked Elvis about his family and friends who had left the Park Hotel and moved to the Grünewald Hotel. Elvis told me that he and his entourage had moved again. He was now living with them in a house in Bad Nauheim.

By then I had figured out that Elvis's family of "dependents" made him eligible to live off post. I had gotten to know the town of Bad Nauheim pretty well and asked him where he lived.

"Fourteen Goatastrass."

Boy, could Elvis butcher the German language! He was trying to say Fourteen Göethestrasse. But I understood what he meant, and I knew that street because our four-year-old daughter, Jill, attended a German kindergarten near there.

Elvis then looked off into the distance and didn't say anything for maybe a half minute. That was a habit of his, and I got to know this faraway gaze much better over time. His thought processes appeared to me to be a bit unusual. He could be animated and smiling that "Elvis smile" at one moment, then switch to a brooding look that appeared to take him a million miles away.

When break time was up and the class started again, I saw Sergeant Jones walk in, lean against the back wall, and light up a cigarette. (There weren't any rules against smoking inside buildings in those days.) After a couple of minutes, I sidled up to Jones and quietly asked him to step outside. He nodded and walked out with me.

"What's with this Presley living off post stuff?" I asked him.

"Well, Sir, *they*, have decided that Elvis has dependents and can live off post." He winced as he said it.

"Why, for Christ's sake? Who are these people?"

Jones looked down and shuffled his feet. He always did that when he was thinking hard.

"His grandmother and his father, plus two bodyguards."

This was beginning to add up. The arrangement surely was legal and in accordance with regulations. If Elvis's father and/or grandmother were carried on the record as his dependents, Elvis could live off post with them. But was it a good idea for Elvis? None of his other unmarried friends could do this. It could surely drive a wedge between him and his platoon.

"Anything can happen anytime. Right, Sarge?"

Jones took a long drag on his cigarette and blew the smoke away hard. "No shit, Sir."

I asked how Elvis was going to get back and forth to the battalion area from Bad Nauheim. Jones paused and grimaced. "Sir, you want to go to Friedberg for a drink after work?"

That was an unusual question because, in general, officers and NCOs didn't spend time drinking together—for lots of reasons. In fact, the chance encounter at the Park Hotel was the first time Jones and I had ever sat down for a drink, except at recon platoon parties, or on an occasional platoon foray to a *Gasthaus* (German restaurant or bar). But the main point for me at the moment was that it didn't seem proper for me to meet with Jones without also meeting with Ed Hart, the platoon leader. After all, it was Ed Hart's platoon, not mine anymore, and I didn't want Hart to think I was interfering.

"Thanks," I told him, "but I've got my wife's parents on my hands, and I have to go home to be with them."

Jones looked around at nothing in particular (his mind obviously racing) and shuffled his feet. "I just want to talk about things, Sir. Okay?"

There was no way I could refuse. Ira Jones had busted his ass to teach me and help me run the best platoon in the world. Although he never knew it, I sometimes felt like he was the older brother I never had. If he wanted to talk, I'd be there. We agreed to leave work early and meet at 4:30 P.M.

We met at a small Gasthaus in the town of Friedberg between our Kaserne and Little Texas. He had arrived just before me and had a big local beer in front of him. I ordered a white wine.

"Well, I ain't never seen nuthin' like this."

Actually, Jones spoke English rather well, with sort of a Southern accent. But he liked to throw in the "ain'ts" just for emphasis, or fun, or both.

I learned that Jones's problem was not that Elvis had been assigned to his platoon; it was the way the assignment had happened. Jones drawled on.

"What the hell is the army comin' to? Jesus, Lieutenant, everybody's into the act on Presley—well, just about everybody."

He told me that the new Headquarters Company commander, Capt. Ed Betts, was the person who first told Jones about Elvis coming to the recon platoon. I remembered that dealing with Betts could be a problem. Betts was competent in armor tactics and maintenance, but he suffered from migraine headaches, which sometimes made him volatile as hell and unpredictable. Maybe he was hassling Jones.

But it was the off-post situation that was really causing heartburn. Jones told me that he had been made responsible for getting Elvis back and forth from his home in Bad Nauheim to the platoon area. Jones had been picking Elvis up in his own car and taking him home. This was surely an unusual situation—an NCO chauffeuring a private! Elvis had just gotten a car, which made things easier—but not much. Elvis had leased a little white BMW, which stood out like a sore thumb when he drove the fifteen to twenty minutes back and forth from Bad Nauheim to our Ray Barracks Kaserne. In the mid-1950s, most Germans near our area couldn't possibly afford a BMW sports car. And we in the military sure as hell couldn't afford one on our low pay.

Jones went on to tell me that the local police were trying to help out Presley's family. They had posted a sign in front of the house on 14 Göethestrasse stating, "Autographs between 7:30 and 8:30 P.M." But teenagers still mobbed the place.

Then Jones explained that only two people in the battalion had Elvis's home phone number—Captain Betts and himself.

"You mean three people, don't you? What about Lieutenant Hart?" I asked. Jones explained that Ed Hart had said he didn't *want* Elvis's private phone number. This was curious; maybe Ed was trying too hard to "keep distance," to not show favoritism to Elvis.

I always felt it was important to keep on hand the phone numbers of all of my people who lived off post, so I could get in touch with them quickly if I needed to. Since our battalion was located in an area through which the Soviet military forces would attack if war broke out, we had to be ready at all times for an alert. And we practiced these alerts without advance notice frequently throughout the year. Our battalion had only a short time to get everything packed up and get seventy-two tanks and a whole bunch of other tracked vehicles, trucks, and jeeps rolling out of the Kaserne headed for our assigned battle positions. I had established the standard operating procedure (SOP) that the entire recon platoon had to be on the road within one hour after the notice from headquarters. I had shortened that time to forty-five minutes when the recon platoon was changed to the scout platoon, because when that reorganization occurred, the platoon lost its heavier equipment—the two light tanks and two armored personnel carriers. That left the scout squad with only jeeps, so we could move faster. The scouts had to be the first ones out, since they served as road guides for the rest of the battalion heading for battle positions.

To notify everyone of the alert, we had a "telephone tree." The battalion duty officer would take the call from higher headquarters, then call all the companies. The companies would alert everyone in their barracks and call their people who lived off post with families. But because the scout platoon had to move faster than any other unit, the battalion duty officer called the scout platoon leader directly at his home off post and the scout platoon in its barracks. The scout platoon leader called the platoon sergeant, who called the three scout section leaders, who also lived off post. The jeep drivers for these leaders, who lived in the barracks (except for Elvis), would race to pick up their bosses and take them to the

Kaserne. In short order, the one lieutenant and thirty-nine enlisted men would be assembled in one place with their fourteen jeeps ready for action.

Strictly speaking, Lieutenant Hart would not need Elvis's private phone number for this alert telephone tree, because Jones, as platoon sergeant, would be responsible for calling Elvis. Still, there were other reasons for platoon leaders to have the phone numbers of their people off post: it was important to keep tabs on their dependents' welfare and to keep open the flow of communications so necessary for unit cohesion—the sense of belonging, the sense of caring about each other. Equally important, there was a plan for the evacuation of dependents if war actually broke out: dependents would be picked up by buses and trucks and taken to the closest airport. How could these things be done for Elvis's dependents if the platoon leader didn't have the private, off-post phone number? Perhaps other arrangements had been made, but this would have been yet another exception to normal policy, and there were already too many exceptions in Elvis's case—too many for his own good. It was in *his* interest to be treated as much as possible like his comrades.

Sergeant Jones broke my stream of thought.

"Damn, Lieutenant, there goes that speed-of-light brain again. What's on your mind now?"

I didn't want to tell Ira Jones that I thought the battalion was off to a very bad start with Elvis Presley. So I just asked him to tell me about Elvis and how he and Lieutenant Hart planned to integrate him into the platoon. It was a sincere question. I knew Jones was a great judge of individual character and unit cohesion and that he would have a good plan from which I could learn something. He was the best teacher I had ever had—except for my father.

"Well, for starters, Elvis is alright."

That told me a lot; Ira Jones reserved the term "alright" for the top cut of people.

"Remember, the odds are against him. I mean, the odds of Elvis bein' able to get along with his fellow soldiers, bein' able to concentrate on learnin' his job, and bein' able to pull his weight in the team are pretty low. We got to keep people off his ass, keep him out of the spotlight, and make him a good, solid soldier."

I thought to myself again how lucky Elvis was to find his way to the scout platoon and Ira Jones, after that false start in D Company.

"You wouldn't expect it in light of his big-time background, but he's calm and he thinks things out. He's pretty damn smart, too. But he ain't a smart-ass."

Hell, Jones really liked the guy! But then, Jones liked all the soldiers in his charge, no matter what their strengths or weaknesses. They were *his*, and he felt responsible for them like they were his own sons. I had always felt the same about my men; that was something I did not have to learn from Ira.

"Elvis is tryin' to do everything right. He's always on time for reveille. He doesn't go home 'til most of the other guys who live off post leave for home. He has all his equipment in tip-top shape—uniforms are just right, tools on the jeep in class-A shape. He tries in every way to be one of the guys, very respectful."

Jones paused, thinking, then asked me how I liked my job as B Company exec. Without telling him how much I missed working with him and the platoon, I explained that I was learning new things, really respected most of our NCOs, and was trying hard to take the load off our company commander.

"You'll be in command of that company soon. You can hack it." This was the same kind of support and confidence Ira gave his men.

I raised my glass, he raised his, and we toasted—victory or death. Laughing together, we drained the last of our drinks.

As I drove home, I thought about what Ira had said, and my initial apprehensions began to ease. Despite all the complications of having Elvis Presley assigned to the battalion, things might work out. Lieutenant Colonel Williams had made the right decision in reassigning Elvis to the best unit in the battalion. Ed Hart and Ira Jones could balance the first priority demands of the mission and the second priority demands of integrating Elvis and his entourage into the 32d Tank Battalion life on post, off post, and in the field.

We were a proud battalion. There was an underlying sense that we could do anything better than any other battalion in the army, and the belief was infectious. There was a very strong unit cohesion—when any one of us got off on the wrong track, everyone else would pull together to set things right. And that's what military unit cohesion is all about: "all for one and one for all."

I remembered what my father told me before I left for Germany in 1956. He was commenting on Japan's new management method, but the point he was making was not all that new.

Hell, Billy, it's common sense about leadership. You just figure out where you want an organization to go; get to know the people who work for, around, and over you; make sure you know their strengths and weaknesses; make sure you get a feel for their fears, hopes, and aspirations; listen carefully to what they say; help them to learn; help them to achieve; persuade them that when the organization achieves, they do and vice-versa; set the example—work harder and smarter than they do; reward their achievements; when something big goes wrong, take the blame, while asking those closest to the problem to help you in a team effort to solve it. And *never, never,* take credit for success yourself!

When I walked in at about 5:45 P.M., Peggy reminded me that I had to pick up our baby-sitter, so I drove the five minutes over to Göethestrasse. As I passed number 14, there stood Elvis in the driveway with the gates open. He had just returned from Ray Barracks. He knew my car and waved for me to stop. He saluted, then asked me to come in to meet his grandma, Minnie Mae.

The house wasn't all that impressive, but it sure was a lot bigger than my two-bedroom apartment in Little Texas. It was a typical three-story German home painted white over cement or stucco. A white picket fence sat atop a concrete base, and the short driveway to the side had white picket gates. The lower windows were covered by what appeared to be pull-down shutters for either privacy or to prevent break-ins, or both. A VW Bug and Elvis's white BMW sports car were parked in the driveway.

He led me through a side door off the driveway and into the kitchen where a lady was cooking. Elvis introduced me to Minnie Mae, a fairly stocky woman in a white blouse and skirt, who seemed to be a very jolly person with a nice smile. She wiped her hands with a kitchen towel and gave me a firm handshake. I told her how nice it was to meet her and went on to say how much we all welcomed Elvis and his family to our battalion family. We exchanged other pleasantries until I excused myself to go pick up our baby-sitter.

On the way out, I thanked Elvis for introducing me to his grandmother. He explained that his father and the friends who lived with him were out, but he hoped that I could meet them sometime soon. I never did. This was the only time I was ever in Elvis's home.

Integrating Elvis, or any other newly assigned young private, took a lot of time and careful attention. The U.S. Army did not rotate entire company or battalion-sized units in which soldiers knew each other well and had trained together, but instead used a system of individual soldier replacements. This meant that a period of socialization and training was needed for new soldiers coming to Germany to replace those whose tour of duty was over.

I had a few opportunities, such as the map-reading class with Sergeant Callender, to observe Elvis in training. One day in mid- or late October, I was down in the B Company maintenance area, close to where the scout platoon was holding one of its frequent drills with the .30-caliber machine guns mounted on their jeeps. I walked over to watch. Although Elvis's HQ31 jeep was designated for the platoon sergeant and did not have a machine gun, all platoon members had to know the drill. In combat, if one member of the platoon were badly wounded or killed, another member might be shifted to take over his position.

It was a fairly cold late fall day. Cold weather generally came early in Germany, and weather reports were forecasting a brutal winter. For the machine-gun drill, you really couldn't wear GI issue gloves, which were olive-drab-colored mittens under a shell of black leather gloves.

Some members of the scout platoon were assembled in team formations in front of their jeeps. Old canvas tarpaulins had been cut up and laid out just behind the men. Elvis was standing in front of one of the machine-gun jeeps with two other guys, Privates Conway and Wittington. Sergeant Jones checked the stopwatch in his hand, then blew a whistle. Elvis turned quickly to his left, took two or three bounding steps, leaped up on the driver's seat, and jumped to the left side of the pedestal-mounted machine gun. He cleared the gun by lifting the bolt cover, pulling back the bolt with the retracting handle, visually verified that there was no round in the chamber, let the bolt slam forward, and pulled the trigger with the barrel pointed up in the air. Conway, who had mounted the right side of the jeep, withdrew the pintal that secured the gun. Elvis grabbed the gun with his left hand holding the barrel and his right hand on the carrying handle. He handed the gun down to Wittington, the third member of the machine-gun jeep crew thrown together for this drill. Wittington quickly moved to the front of the jeep and placed the gun on the tarpaulin. Then Elvis, who had quickly dismounted, kneeled down and began to disassemble the gun. He flipped up the breech cover again, grabbed a screwdriver, turned a screw that secured the bolt-driving spring, let the spring out slowly and removed it, lifted the base and pistol grip group away from the gun's main breech, snapped the bolt back and out of the breech, laid it on the tarpaulin next to the spring, checked the belt-fed pawl, and then shouted "up" as he quickly withdrew his hands to his sides.

Jones clicked his stopwatch, saying, "Okay, stand easy. That was ten seconds too damn long. Conway, don't climb up the backside of the jeep, just step on the seat with your right foot and into the back with your left. When you slipped coming over the right rear, you coulda' broken your leg and, anyway, it cost you some seconds. By the way, you moved about as quick as my granny."

The rest of the platoon started chuckling and ragging Conway. "Yeah, Granny Conway sounds about right." "Want a cane, Granny?"

"Okay, knock it off," said Jones. "Now, Wittington, you hit the damn windshield frame when you came around toward the tarp. Damn near broke the thing. That's a machine gun you're totin', not a magic wand. You ain't the fairy godmother, ya' know."

From someone else in the crowd came, "Yeah, he's a fairy, Sarge. Don't ya' know?"

Another sergeant got in a shot, saying "You outta know, queer bait." Howls of laughter came from the rest of the platoon.

"Okay, okay. Now Elvis, you gotta get the motion with that spring. It took you too long to unseat the holding screw and too long to retract. You can't be too fast though, or that spring is gonna fly out and knock your balls off. Here, let me show you." Jones got down on his knees and reassembled the gun like greased lightning. Then he said, "Now all you guys watch this."

Jones moved his hands with precision. He picked up the screwdriver, moved his wrist slightly to the left, and eased out the spring in an easy but quick motion.

Elvis just said, "Okay, I got it."

I noticed that no one was ragging Elvis. He was too new in the platoon, and the guys didn't want to take a chance on hurting his feelings. This was part of good platoon socialization. Jones cautioned everyone in the platoon to be kind to the new guys until they were thoroughly integrated into the team. Then he would say, "Once a guy's solidly part of the team, I don't give a shit what you say or do to each other."

The old recon platoon team was famous for its horseplay, and I was sure it was the same in the scout platoon. Guys would play tricks on each other all the time in garrison, like short sheeting each other's bunks, or setting up a guy's wall locker so that everything rolled out like Fibber McGee's closet when the locker door was opened. Another favorite was a bucket of cold water on a guy taking a hot shower. It was all in good fun, never designed to hurt a buddy or his feelings.

Even though the mix of people in the unit changed as men were reassigned and new men took their places, the unit cohesion always remained solidly intact, mainly because of Jones's leadership. It's no exaggeration to say these guys loved each other and would sacrifice for each other. Elvis quickly became an integral part of all this. As I observed him periodically, I could see this happening: Elvis was becoming one of the elite scouts of the 32d Tank Battalion.

"Okay, Sarge, let's go again," said Elvis.

"Okay, okay, positions," barked Jones. He held out his stopwatch, put his whistle in his mouth, then blew hard. The crew scrambled. When Elvis was finished, he yelled "up" and dropped his hands to his sides.

"Well, umm, not bad, not bad. In fact, that time's gonna be hard to beat."

"We can beat it, Sarge. Let's go again, we're hot!" exclaimed Elvis. There is no doubt that Elvis Presley was a real competitor, as I was to see time and time again over the following months.

"Na. You'll have plenty of chances later. Okay, who's ready?" queried Jones. Another team of three quickly walked over to the same machine-gun jeep.

"Okay, Presley, put that thing back together. Conway, you put the gun back on the pedestal. Let's go, let's go. We ain't got all day," said Jones, clapping his big strong hands for emphasis.

I went back to my own business, spot checking maintenance records for B Company's seventeen big 90mm gun tanks. We had a battalion maintenance inspection coming up soon, and I wasn't about to lose points on paper records, much less anything having to do with the actual condition of our main combat power.

Maybe a week or so later, I watched Elvis at an early-morning physical training (PT) formation. The scout platoon had formed up in the street in front of their barracks near the "Wild Wolf" platoon sign.

It was cold outside. I had just returned from running with B Company and was still sweating under my fatigue jacket. Before going in to clean up, I sat on the front steps and watched the scout platoon.

They had on their fatigue jackets and gloves. It was a pain in the butt to take PT with so much gear on, but there was no choice. When the snows and freezing rains of winter came, we'd have to take PT inside at the Combat Command gym, which meant PT would be held at whatever time of the day you could get your unit on the gym's schedule.

I saw Ed Hart starting to put the platoon through its paces. First, a few minutes of jumping jacks to loosen up. Then a couple of minutes to rest. Next came a series of "squat thrusts," a four-count exercise where you stood at attention, squatted down, put your hands on the ground, thrust your legs out behind you into a push-up position, pulled your knees back up under the chest, and stood up quickly into the position of attention.

I noticed that Hart had the platoon lined up by height, with the tallest guys on the left. At about six feet and one or two inches, Elvis stood third in the front rank after Sergeant Jones and Pfc. Pat Conway.

Hart let the platoon rest a couple of minutes after the squat thrusts, then called the formation to attention. "Okay, thirty push-ups. Platoon, attenhut! Ready, exercise. One, two, three . . ."

I focused on the push-ups. You could always tell who was dogging it in PT by watching the push-ups. Did a guy skip a cadence every so often? Was he going all the way down to touch his chest? Did he lock his arms straight in the up position? Did he have his ass up in the air, or did he keep a stiff, straight frame with each count?

I watched Elvis knock off thirty push-ups with perfect precision. Hart, in the up position, arms locked, said, "Okay, you overachievers, keep on going." Maybe half the platoon stood up. The other half, including Elvis, kept on pumping. As each guy reached his limit, he stood up. Sergeant Kennedy was the next to last up, and Elvis was still pumping at about sixty or so. Hart said, "Okay, Presley, good. You qualify for the Olympics. Loosen up guys and let's run."

After a couple more minutes, Hart gave the appropriate orders: "Platoon, attenhut! Right face! Forward march! Double time, march!" And off went the platoon down the main battalion road, past the motor pool, and out the back gate. I could hear Hart chanting some double-time "Jody cadence" as they ran, with the platoon chanting in unison at the right junctures.

They would be gone for at least twenty minutes, so I walked back into our headquarters to clean up in the bathroom. I was heading for battalion headquarters when the scout platoon returned from their run and "fell out" of formation.

"Hey, Ed, not bad for an old man," I teased. Ed was maybe a year older than I.

"Bill, how's it going? Peggy ready for number three, yet?" We shot the breeze for a minute, then Ed headed for the Headquarters Company area.

Elvis was standing with Kennedy, jibing about who could do more push-ups.

"Sarge, I stopped just so you wouldn't look so bad."

"El, I coulda' kept on to a hundred but thought I'd let you feel good about doin' sumthin' right for a change."

"Oh, bullshit," Elvis said with a half-amused, half-surprised look, as he whipped off his hat and slapped it on his knee, looking like a baseball team manager yelling at an umpire about a call he didn't like.

It was obviously all in fun—the kind of horseplay that happens between people who respect and like each other. Yes, Elvis definitely was part of the scout platoon team.

I walked toward them, and they came to attention with smart salutes. I knew Kennedy well: he was one of the older members of my former platoon. He was a tough, powerful guy with a good sense of humor. No one outside the platoon screwed around with him. He had a reputation as one tough dude, who could rip your head off if you crossed him. He was also a real competitor and had made his stripes pretty fast. It made me feel good that Kennedy and Elvis got along so well.

"How you doin', Sir," said Kennedy.

"Hey Lootenet, how's the family? Your folks still here?"

"No, Peggy's parents stayed two weeks and left for Paris. I saw you two guys at PT. You look like you're in good shape."

"All in the mind, Sir, all in the mind," said Kennedy with a big grin.

"No quitters around here, Lootenet. This team don't quit."

"Yes, well, keep up the good work. The whole battalion is proud of you guys," I said, saluting as I turned to head over to battalion headquarters.

One final incident led me to conclude that Elvis was fully integrated into his platoon and the 32d. It was right after the first snowfall, a raw, cold, windy day. It was definitely a day for indoor classes, but my company exec had called me about a problem with my command tank and wanted me to come talk it over with him and the maintenance NCO. For whatever reason, a crack had opened up in the base of the carburetor. Three carburetors had been on back order for weeks from our direct support ordnance company, and the word was that nothing was due through the pipeline for some time. This was getting to be a big problem for the entire battalion. Our equipment was starting to get "deadlined" in worrisome numbers, as operations and maintenance funds were slashed by declining annual defense budgets. I needed to go talk about some creative solutions, especially in relation to my command tank.

As I crossed the battalion street, there came Elvis heading in the same direction toward the motor pool. He had the earflaps down on his winter fur-felt cap, tied under his chin. We saluted, and he asked me what was up. I told him about the problem.

"Hell," said Elvis, "we're feelin' the same pinch in the platoon. We can't get parts either. How in hell do they expect us to be combat ready when we gotta deadline jeeps? We even got a machine gun deadlined because the armorer can't replace a puny broken belt-fed pawl. Can't get a replacement for a broken lens in my own binoculars either."

"So what are you going to do?" I asked.

"Right now, I'm gonna see if I can get somebody in headquarters maintenance to weld the pawl and grind off the rough edges. Might be able to get it to work until a new piece comes in."

"Actually, I've got the same thing in mind for the carb on my tank. Maybe we can disassemble the thing and weld the crack, depending on where the crack is. Maybe good old 'field expedients' will work here. We'll see. Have to do something. I'll be damned if I'm going to leave a tank behind in the motor pool if we get the word to move out."

We walked with our heads bent, leaning into the wind with snow blowing at our faces. "You all settled in with the platoon? Any problems?"

"Lootenet, you were right at the Park Hotel—these guys are great. I mean really great. Not an asshole in the crowd. We can really count on each other. I feel like I've known 'em for a long time. The Lord was watchin' out for me again when I left D Company."

"Lieutenant Hart tells me that he's heading back to the States pretty soon and that Sergeant Jones will be the acting platoon leader for the indefinite future. How do you feel about that?"

We were just walking up to the headquarters company maintenance bay, and Elvis said, "Come on in for a minute? Let's get out of this shit." I nodded agreement, and we walked into the bay area warmed by oil-fired stoves.

Elvis answered my question. "Well, we'll miss Lootenet Hart, but as long as 'ol Ira' is with us, everything will be good. They say that we got him until April—same time they say you'll be headin' out. That right?"

"Yes, Jones and I both are scheduled to depart sometime in April."

"Well, Lootenet, we just ain't gonna worry about anything until April."

Elvis looked around. We both could see that there was only one person in the place. "Where is everybody?" Elvis asked the maintenance records clerk.

The guy told Elvis that the maintenance section was having a periodic review of its personnel records; everybody was at the battalion personnel office, and he had to hightail it over there also. Elvis asked if he could stay until they got back because he had something to fix. The guy agreed and left.

I told Elvis that I had to get over to my company maintenance area (which was only about fifty yards away). He said, "Okay, Sir, stop back by if you got time."

I went back out into the wind and snow and walked over to my own maintenance bays. I walked into a beehive of activity.

There sat tank B6, my command tank, with the big iron grates that cover the engine compartment pulled back.

"Okay, what's up?" I asked.

My maintenance sergeant explained that they were going to try to weld the crack. Hello, these guys were already ahead of me.

"Well, let me know ASAP what happens. How about a rundown on our stuff. Just give me the real problems," I said.

As it turned out, tank B21 was deadlined for a broken torsion bar. The torsion bar is a device in a tank or other heavy vehicle that takes the place of normal shock absorbers. The maintenance NCO couldn't get one through the routine parts process, so he had dispatched a mechanic to get one outside the system.

"What is it going to cost us?" I asked.

He grinned. "A bottle of bourbon and the gas it takes to get to Gelnhausen."

"How much is the bourbon?" I asked.

"Kinda' good stuff, Sir, four bucks."

I reached into my pocket, pulled out some bills, and peeled off four one-dollar scrip notes. "Fair price," I said. "Good thinking, Sarge."

Four bucks was a lot of money in those days, and I hoped the goddamn supply system would work a little better before April.

"Anything else?" I asked.

"Naw. Not if we can weld this carb and make it work."

"Okay, you guys are doing a great job as usual. Keep it up."

I left, this time with the wind and snow at my back, and walked to the headquarters maintenance area. The door blew shut behind me. Elvis was leaning over a steel bench with a welding torch in his hands and welder's goggles propped up on his forehead.

"This fucking thing is driving me fucking crazy," he complained in about as frustrated a tone as I had ever heard. "I can't get the flame right."

Having worked as a welder's apprentice one summer, I knew more than a little about welding, both acetylene and arc. "Let me see the thing, okay?"

"Sure, Lootenet."

I checked the control valves on both the acetylene and the oxygen tanks and found the oxygen valve was not fully open. I opened it to the max, then adjusted the two knobs controlling the flow to the torch.

"Okay if I do it?"

Elvis said, "Sure, thanks."

"Goggles?"

Elvis handed them to me, and I pulled them on with one hand, holding the torch with the other. I looked at the flame on the torch. It was close in at the tip, blue with a tiny fraction of an inch of yellow flame just beyond the blue. Perfect.

Elvis mumbled, "You done this before?"

"Yeah, I have. Looks like you have the broken pawl pieces perfectly aligned in the vice. Just right—good job."

I picked up a welding rod and, putting the tip of the rod adjacent to both the broken parts of the pawl and the torch flame, laid a small bead on the break amid a few sparks.

"Hey, Elvis [I realized that I had never used his first name, and I wished I hadn't then], some water." He picked up a hydrometer and squeezed out a few drops on the weld. It hissed and smoked.

"Other side?"

Elvis loosened the vice, turned over the pawl, and tightened it back up. I repeated the procedure on the reverse side and the two other corners.

"Okay," I said. Elvis grabbed hold of the pawl with pliers, loosened the vice, and plunged the hot metal into a can of water.

"Looks damn good. I'll grind it down. Okay, Lootenet?"

"Okay, great." I turned off the torch knobs, then the tank controls.

Elvis turned on a bench grinder and carefully ground down the welds to match the original contour of the little pawl shaft. Then he put the pawl back in the vice, got out a file, and started to do the final shaping.

About that time the headquarters maintenance crew came back. The sergeant looked at what Elvis was doing, then said, "Hell, El, that's one hell of a weld. Good job."

Elvis just said "Thanks" and let it go at that. Then he muttered, "Well, all the bluin's gone. Gonna have to oil this thing a lot, but it's gonna work."

Elvis hung up the torch and put away the tools. "You ready to go, Lootenet?"

"Sure. I've got a lot to do this afternoon before I hang it up," I said.

Before we opened the door to walk back out into the elements, Elvis asked, "Is there anything you can't do, Lootenet?"

My reply was instantaneous, "Yes, my friend, I cannot play the guitar, I cannot sing rock 'n' roll, and I'm not sure I can do as many push-ups as you. Well, actually, I probably can do more push-ups than you."

Elvis grinned. "Wanna try sometime?"

"Hell yes, but not now," I groaned, as we stepped out into the cold.

I had to shout across the wind blowing at our backs. "You're a good man, Presley." We saluted as best we could with our field jacket hoods up around our heads.

That afternoon was meaningful to me: to see Elvis Presley there, on his own accord, working to help out his unit, told me that he was now one very well integrated, very competitive, and fine member of the 32d Tank Battalion team.

CHAPTER 4

GETTING TO KNOW ELVIS

E lvis's daily routine at Ray Barracks was the same as that of everyone else in the platoon who lived off post. The scout platoon was very different from the four tank companies of the battalion, and the training for scouts encompassed the large number of diverse tasks that could be assigned at the drop of a hat. But a typical day in garrison for Elvis might be as follows:

6:30 A.M.—out the door from home to drive in POV (privately owned vehicle) from Bad Nauheim, through the town of Friedberg, to Ray Barracks.

6:50 to 7:00 A.M.—report for duty in the scout platoon building. The on-post troops had already had morning chow.

7:00 A.M.—platoon formation, followed by police call (picking up any trash around the area).

7:15 A.M.—form up for PT.

7:45 A.M.—back to the barracks to cool off or warm up, depending on the weather. Straighten out wall lockers and footlockers where combat gear is stored.

8:00 A.M.—first class of the day. For scouts, this could be map reading, route and area reconnaissance, bridge classification, or any number of other scout specialties.

9:45 A.M.—break for relaxation or personal affairs.

10:00 A.M.—second class. For scouts this might be weapons disassembly, cleaning, and assembly; theory of weapons firing; or vehicle maintenance procedures.

11:45 A.M.—break (Elvis and some of the NCOs often drove home for a fast lunch).

12:00 P.M.—noon chow.

1:00 P.M.—motor pool for vehicle maintenance.

2:45 P.M.—break.

3:00 P.M.—TI&E (troop information and education) class on current events, civil-military relations, German-American relations or the like.

4:00 P.M.—break.

4:15 P.M.—radio communications, maintenance, or repair. Or CBR (chemical, biological, and radiological-warfare training).

5:30 P.M.—head for home.

There were frequent exceptions to this garrison schedule, especially when we had to prepare our equipment for special inspections—and there were more kinds than you could imagine. That meant maintenance sessions that could last late into the night or even all night. Like the rest of the 32d Tank Battalion units, the scout platoon had to be prepared for the unexpected.

As it turned out, Elvis and I sometimes came across each other in the battalion area several times a day. A battalion of 750 people sounds like a lot, but we were around each other almost 365 days a year and lots of nights, either preparing for inspections or working around the Kaserne or out in the field on practice maneuvers. The 32d Tank Battalion area wasn't all that big—about two square city blocks plus the tank park and fuel and ammunition storage areas. And, because we were a tank battalion, we all spent lots of time "pulling maintenance" in the battalion maintenance area or in the tank park, where the seventy-two tanks (at fifty tons each), a dozen or so armored personnel carriers, and assorted other track and wheeled vehicles were parked.

Those tanks were our reason for existing. The mission was to be prepared twenty-four hours a day to get those babies to the right place at the right time to close with and kill the Soviet enemy in combat. The first part of that mission was to keep the tanks running and ready to shoot their 90mm main guns. Believe me, keeping cars or trucks running in tip-top shape is a cakewalk compared with tanks.

As a tank company executive officer, vehicle maintenance was my first responsibility. Most execs hated the task. I loved it, but then I loved everything about my job. Well, except for a few minor regulations. And I loved everything to do with motor vehicles. Elvis and I were to discover that we both loved hot cars, but more on that later.

So I spent a lot of time with our soldiers in the motor pool, trying my best to teach them how to do their jobs and to *like* doing their jobs. In my constant treks between the B Company tank line, the battalion maintenance office, the B Company barracks, and battalion headquarters, I ran into Elvis often. He worked on his (Sergeant Jones's) jeep all the time—washing, lubricating, changing oil or filter, greasing chassis joints, checking or cleaning communications radios, checking tire pressure, cleaning OVM (on vehicle maintenance) tools, cleaning, sharpening, and painting pioneer tools (shovel and ax), and so on. This upkeep was not something done once in a while; it was an ongoing task to keep combat vehicles ready to go.

One day I was walking by the scout platoon parking area when I saw jeep HQ31 jacked up on one side with a pair of booted feet sticking out from underneath. There were no jack stands under the side, just a jack. That was unstable and dangerous as hell to whoever was under the jeep. HQ31; it had to be Elvis. I squatted down.

"Soldier, would you slide out here for a minute?"

"Wait a minute, I got to pull a branch outta' here."

I waited, and out wriggled Elvis. He stood up, brushed off his fatigue uniform, and smiled.

"Hi, Wild—I mean Lootenet." Soldiers generally didn't stand at attention or salute in the motor pool working area, but they also didn't call an officer by his nickname. So Sgt. Bob Hodges's legacy was still with me. Hodges had given me the nickname "Wild Bill" Taylor, and it had become part of the recon and now the scout platoon's lore.

I stuck out my hand to shake Elvis's greasy palm.

"Good to see you again, Presley. If you want to keep your body in one piece, don't ever get under a jacked-up vehicle unless the wheels are chocked on both sides and you have jack stands under the frame."

I asked him to walk over to the Headquarters Company maintenance area and sign out two jack stands. He was gone only about five minutes.

"You know how to use these things?"

"Sure do, Lootenet." He wound the jack up a few turns, pushed the stands in under the jeep side frame, and let the jack down.

"How's that, Lootenet?"

"How about the chocks?"

Elvis smiled again. "Well, actually, I already finished the job. I just wanted to show you that I know how to do it right."

He put his greasy hands in the pockets of his dirty fatigues and stood there, still smiling. I smiled back, and finally we both broke out laughing.

I saluted him. "Presley, you're something else."

"You too, Lootenet. Lootenet, where'd ya' get the nickname?"

"What nickname?" (As if I didn't know.)

"You know—'Wild Bill,'" said Elvis, shuffling his feet and looking embarrassed like a kid asking his parents a question about sex.

"Well, Sergeant Hodges gave it to me."

"Tell me some more about Hodges. I hear stuff about him all the time. Sergeant Jones tells me that Hodges knows more about recon than any guy in the army."

"You'd better believe it. Hodges is crazy as hell, but he's a pro."

"Well, every time we have classes somebody brings up something about how Sergeant Hodges did it."

"Okay, let's take a break," I said. We leaned up against the side of HQ31. I wanted a cigarette—I'd started smoking again—but you couldn't smoke in the motor pool area where gas, oil, and welding tanks were used and stored.

"It was a long time ago. I was the recon platoon leader, and Hodges and I were performing a route reconnaissance out ahead of two companies of the battalion. Sergeant Jones was a mile or so away with one scout section, doing the same thing on another parallel road for two other tank companies. Along my route, there was an old, masonry-arch bridge over a twenty-meter-wide river that was swollen and rushing along because of heavy rains."

"Was it night or day?" asked Elvis.

"Night. The two tank companies were approaching the bridge on a lights-out, night march at about ten miles per hour. There wasn't any satisfactory alternate route for them, and the entire battalion had only another forty-five minutes to reach the line of departure for a simulated attack."

"Jones always says that bein' late to the LD is a tactical sin in a combat unit."

"That's right. Well, I had to make a decision on whether that little bridge would carry thirty-four tanks in succession without breaking up. There was no possibility of fording, because the rain had made the river too deep and too fast. I had to make a fast decision and radio it to the battalion commander— at that time Lieutenant Colonel Stark. Whatever I said, he would trust. If I was wrong, not only would the bridge cave in, but a tank crew might die."

"Damn," uttered Elvis.

"It was cold, but I was sweating. I took out my 'bridge stress calculation chart,' made the proper measurements by eyeball, and ran the mathematical calculations in my head. Sergeant Hodges was leading the one scout section that was with me. What you've heard is true, Hodges was the best NCO in the division when it came to route reconnaissance. So, not being a total fool, I turned to Hodges for advice. I told him that I thought we could make it if the tanks crossed at about three miles per hour."

"What'd he say?" Elvis was listening intently, evidently conjuring up the scene in his mind.

"'Aw, no problem,' Hodges said, with such confidence that I began to wonder why I had any doubt. So I radioed Colonel Stark and told him that the bridge was passable on a risk crossing."

Elvis nodded in the affirmative, so I assumed he knew what "risk crossing" meant. It meant that tank gun loaders would have to dismount from each tank before it crossed the bridge and, using a "masked" flashlight (with a plastic shield permitting only a dull glow), lead the tank driver *slowly* across this very narrow bridge. A tank does not exert much ground pressure because the weight is spread out over the long, wide tracks. But at too high a speed, they "shake, rattle, and roll," which could cause an old masonry-arch bridge to collapse.

I continued the story. "Hodges and I waited to see the bridge crossing. When the B Company lead tank got to the bridge, the loader dismounted and led the driver across the bridge—very slowly. After the first platoon of five tanks had made it across, I was confident that everything would be okay."

Elvis nodded again.

"Hodges and I took our jeeps to a piece of high ground where we were to rendezvous with the rest of the platoon to set up a recon screen out on the battalion's left flank. When we arrived at the right spot, we stopped and dismounted. Hodges lit a cigarette under his poncho, held the cigarette in the cup of his hand, and puffed. I called the D Company commander and found that both companies had cleared the bridge."

"That must have felt pretty good, after not being sure."

"Yes, for a couple of seconds. But then Hodges piped up with, 'Wild Bill, you sure got balls. There's a big crack down the middle of that bridge's arch.' I had not seen the crack in the darkness, and that arrogant, semidisrespectful, little son of a bitch had let me take one big risk without telling me a thing. And then he stuck the needle in a little more by saying that he had always wondered whether that bridge would take a tank! And, of course, Hodges loved telling the story later. But I also found out later that Hodges had actually seen tanks cross that bridge before and was confident we could make it, despite the crack."

"Damn," said Elvis, "that was a pretty big decision. They tell me that Hodges was the best."

"He was indeed," I said, shaking my head.

Elvis changed the subject. "So that's where 'Wild Bill' comes from. Do you mind, Lootenet?"

"No, I don't mind. And I miss having Hodges around. He was one of a kind." I turned and hadn't gone more than a few steps when Elvis walked up behind me.

"Sure heard a lot about you from the guys, Lootenet. Glad to be with ya'."

I threw him a salute; he returned it with his greasy right hand. We smiled warmly at each other again, and I left. The love I felt for the guys in that platoon had been returned repeatedly in many ways. "Glad to be with ya'" was just another way.

A day or so later I ran into Elvis again by chance in the motor pool. I was walking out of the B Company maintenance bay to go back to the B Company headquarters. As I turned the corner, there was Elvis, crouched in karate form, palms in striking posture, circling an "opponent." He moved forward, then spun around, extending a stiff-legged kick (which pulled up short of the other guy), and yelled, "Hee-yah!"

I exclaimed, "What in hell is this, the local gym?" Actually, I had heard that Elvis had begun taking private karate lessons from a German instructor.

The two of them stopped their little exercise, looking embarrassed, like two little kids caught with their hands in the cookie jar.

"Oh, just limberin' up, Lootenet."

He started to salute, then seemed to recall that we normally did not salute in the motor pool. "Gotta get back to work," he said.

"Me too," I replied.

The three of us exchanged waves and went our different ways.

Thereafter, whenever Elvis and I passed each other in the motor pool, we always waved and smiled. His smile just lit up his face—it was infectious. I wondered why his photographs often portrayed such a brooding expression.

When he was with others from the scout platoon, I would often stop and shoot the breeze. I was always sensitive to the fact that I was no longer the platoon leader, but I just couldn't manage to distance myself too far. That would have been like divorcing a family.

Elvis heard the personal stuff the guys and I shared. They always asked about "Mrs. T, Little Jill, and Tod." And I asked about their families and about what was going on in their lives. We talked about the unforgettable times we had shared, and about their hopes and fears for the future. I had spent literally *thousands* of hours training with these men, and I really cared about them. Elvis was neither blind nor insensitive, and the sense of camaraderie we had in the platoon was not lost on him. So he was never distant; Elvis Presley was becoming a real part of the team.

The next time I met Elvis in a one-on-one situation was on the day after an incident at our Kaserne. I was pulling a twenty-four-hour tour of duty as the Combat Command C duty officer. The entire 3d Armored Division was divided into three combat commands in those days. The 32d was part of Combat Command C (CCC) in Friedberg. All the officers were on a duty roster and their names would come up about every three months. When one of us got "the duty" he was responsible for the security of the entire combat command in the Friedberg Kaserne. Another duty roster assigned an officer to be responsible for a mobile "courtesy patrol" in the town of Friedberg.

On the night that I was duty officer, four German teenagers, three girls and one guy, decided that they were going to see Elvis Presley. Someone had told them, or maybe they just assumed, that Elvis lived on post in our Kaserne. They decided to drive to Friedberg from their homes in Frankfurt, find Ray Barracks, break into the Kaserne, and find him. They must have known better than to try to get through the two military policemen at the main gate because they decided to tackle the fence. The fence was about eight feet tall with barbed wire rolled over the top, so they went *under* the fence at a spot where it wasn't properly staked to the ground. Avoiding the walking guard who patrolled that portion of the fence, the kids found their way into the central area.

I was just leaving the duty officer's office to check that all the guards were awake and doing their jobs properly, when I saw the kids walking across a Kaserne street. I asked in English what they were doing. One of them said, "Elvis?" I asked them to come into the headquarters building, called in the German translator who was there every night, and explained to them that Elvis was not around. But the four of them were obsessed with finding Elvis. They pleaded with me.

I looked them directly in the eyes. "Honestly, please believe me, Elvis is not here, and I cannot tell you where he is."

They looked very disappointed. I told them (via translator) that Elvis was trying to be a good soldier for two years, not a rock star; he wanted his privacy, and they should respect that.

One of the girls kept staring at me. "You talk like my older brother," she said. I asked what her brother's job was.

"He's a military leader."

She told me her brother was a company commander in a German unit about halfway between Frankfurt and Friedberg. I asked his name. She hesitated, then told me. I knew the name right away because we sometimes trained with that unit. I wondered what her brother would say if he knew that his little sister had broken into a Kaserne to look for Elvis Presley.

I asked the four whether they would like a truck to drive them somewhere. The guy looked very serious, then smiled sadly and said, "*Ja, bitte.*" My NCOIC (noncommissioned officer in charge) got our light truck and took the four of them to the village of Friedberg, not far from the front gate, where they had parked their car in front of a Gasthaus.

By regulations, I had to write up the incident in the duty officer's log, but I didn't list any of the teenagers' names. Why bring trouble for those kids? The local German police checked every morning with our Kaserne security people to find out about any problems. As fate would have it, I did see the German girl's lieutenant brother a couple of weeks later, but I never mentioned the incident to him.

The next day Ira Jones telephoned me in the early afternoon to say that Elvis wanted to see me.

"Sir, the word's out on the incident last night, and Elvis just wants to talk with you. Okay?"

If something was important to Jones, it became important to me. So I agreed to meet them at the entrance to the maintenance area.

We all exchanged salutes.

"Lootenet, sorry about what happened last night. This kind of pain-in-the-ass happens. I got a few problems—"

I moved fast to cut off his apology. After all, Elvis hadn't caused the problem; the circumstances had. I took a few minutes to tell him that no sane person would blame him. I knew he wanted to apologize for causing *me* problems as duty officer, but I wouldn't let him. In my view, it wouldn't be a good thing for Elvis's sense of self-worth as a soldier to let him blame himself for every problem his fame caused.

As time went on, there were other similar incidents, and I wondered if Elvis blamed himself for these as well. For example, whenever the 32d planned to move out of the Kaserne on a road march, the word always spread, and fans would try to track down Elvis. Soldiers obviously told their wives or German girlfriends where we were going, when we would leave, and when we would probably return. And we had to tell the German employees who worked on the post in various support jobs so they could adjust work plans while we were gone. Everyone knew that the first unit out of the gate would be the scout platoon, with a mission of posting road guides at critical intersections where the battalion's vehicle drivers might make wrong turns. That, of course, meant that Elvis Presley would be out of the Kaserne and somewhere on a road. So help me, the local girls had an intelligence network that was almost infallible. They were like humming birds attracted to a flower. They could almost always find Elvis, and their presence almost always disrupted scout platoon road march operations.

Here's a typical case. In early 1959, the battalion was going to Grafenwöhr for maneuvers. We loaded the tanks on railroad flatcars at a railhead behind our Kaserne area. Road marching (driving) tanks 110 miles put too much wear and tear on them and used too much fuel; also, the fifty-ton beasts tore up the roads. While the track vehicles went by train, most of the battalion's soldiers traveled to Graf by truck and jeep. We would then pick up our tanks and perform our weeks of training maneuvers over hundreds of square miles of open terrain and dirt roads.

In the early morning, an hour before the battalion's main body was to leave, I could see the scout platoon going out the main gate. The route was to the east, toward Czechoslovakia. We would follow the roads south to Offenbach, then east through Aschaffenburg, Würzburg (where we often stayed overnight), Kitzingen, Bamberg, and Bayreuth to Grafenwöhr. The first time I saw Elvis getting thronged by girls was just outside the town of Würzburg, about halfway between our

Friedberg Kaserne and Graf. We had spent the night at a U.S. military unit's parade field, and first thing the next morning we resumed our road march. B Company was in the lead that day, and I was riding in the lead company jeep. It was cold, with a light snow falling. As soon as I got out the front gate, I saw a horde of young girls jumping up and down, waving notepads in their hands, and pressing in on a jeep. You've got it; the jeep was HQ31, Sergeant Jones's vehicle, and his driver, Elvis Presley, was the center of attention. How did they know it was Elvis? They must have been looking for the jeep number stenciled in white on the olive-drab bumper. Surely the girls could not have identified Elvis himself. It was so cold that we had the tops and doors on our jeeps, and we all wore fur caps with earflaps down and tied around our chins. No matter; they found him. They always did.

I radioed my 1st Platoon leader, telling him that I was dropping out to check on something, and that he would be the lead company jeep until I rejoined the column. He gave me a "Wilco, Six" (meaning, "I understand and will comply"). I pulled over to the right side of the road and asked my driver to back up very slowly—the snow was falling a bit more heavily, reducing visibility. I opened the canvas-and-plastic jeep door and dismounted (tank units considered themselves heirs to the U.S. Cavalry, so you didn't "get out" of a tank or jeep, you "dismounted"). I spotted Ira Jones's tall, lanky frame, and we held up our mittened palms to greet each other.

About twenty-five American and German teenage girls were screaming at the sight of Elvis. The American girls must have been the daughters of U.S. military families living in Würzburg, and I supposed that the German girls were their friends. Jones had obviously told Elvis to give the kids a signature, and that is what he was doing.

I asked Jones why he had stopped near the Würzburg PX area with Elvis, since it was a place where he could easily be spotted.

"Well, Lieutenant Hart took the lead, positioning the platoon, and I took the base."

In our platoon's military jargon, "the base" meant establishing the start point—the line of departure for the battalion's next move. Hart had put Jones there and led the scout platoon on the rest of the route, dropping off vehicles and the platoon's thirty-five or thirty-six road guides at important intersections along the way. This was sound, routine planning. Sound, that is, except for the fact that Elvis was positioned with Sergeant Jones near the Würzburg complex. It would have been better to put Jones and Elvis out on the road in the most isolated area. But perhaps he had his own reasons for what he did.

Sergeant Jones glowered at me. "Do you think the base is established?" He was asking if all the companies were flowing well enough that he could get the hell out of there.

"Why not tell Lieutenant Hart that the start point is secure, the main body is flowing, and that, in my opinion, you can move forward."

I never—not once—gave Ira Jones an order. I suggested things. If he didn't agree, he'd say so.

He gave me a nod, went to his jeep radio, and talked with Hart. Then he put down the receiver and ambled over to me. "We're movin'."

I wondered what Elvis thought about all this. He was aware that he had a military mission, and I knew he wanted to do his best. But he also must have thought about the fact that he was going back to stardom once he left the army. I looked over at Elvis, standing next to his jeep, surrounded by his fans. It was pretty cold, but he had pulled off his fur cap; he was smiling at the girls with those eyes, that mouth, and with a charm that was his only. I had never witnessed a scene like this—everyone pushing, shoving, and shouting to get a star's autograph. Elvis was handling it well by all appearances. I heard him say things such as, "Hold it there, honey. Get right to ya', darlin'."

I walked over. "Presley, can you bring this to a happy conclusion?"

He looked at me and yelled over the mostly blond heads. "Damn right, Lootenet. What are we doing here anyway?"

That was my own question.

"No problem. You and Jones know how to get people moving. You got trapped for a few minutes. Now let's move out."

Elvis looked at Jones—the guy who gave him his orders. "Movin' out?"

"Crank it up," said Jones.

Elvis jammed his fur cap back on, letting the long earflaps dangle. Like the rest of us, he looked like a hound dog when the earflaps were not tied under his chin. He shifted his M1 rifle from his left shoulder to his right, waved at the throng of girls, jogged over to his jeep, opened the canvas-and-plastic door, and slid in, wedging his rifle next to the backseat. He turned on the ignition and cranked and cranked, trying to turn over the engine. The damn thing wouldn't start! Over came the girls, surrounding the jeep and yelling, "Elvis! Elvis!" What a pitiful sight. I couldn't help laughing.

I knew that Ira Jones's jeep could not be out of gas. It was an "iron law" that *all* vehicles must be topped off with gas before the end of a day's operations. The problem was probably the choke setting or a stuck choke valve. I walked over and yelled for Elvis to turn off the ignition. Asking some of the girls to move over, I unlatched and raised the front hood. I unsnapped a couple of clamps and removed the air cleaner. I could see that the throttle valve was all the way open, so I placed my left palm over the top of the carburetor and yelled for Elvis to try it again. I let it crank over a few times, then opened my palm slightly to let air be sucked in. The engine caught, and Elvis raced it a few times. I put the air cleaner back on, reset the holddown clamps, and lowered the hood. Jones and I signaled with our arms for the girls to move away. They were yelling, "*Bitte, bitte*—please, please." Jones climbed back in his seat. I heard a muffled "thanks" as HQ31 pulled away.

I walked back toward my jeep, ready for the routine work of a very cold day, with many hours ahead of me before we arrived at Graf. A couple of the girls were next to my jeep, talking with my driver, Mac. One of them, a good-looking blond with a knit cap pulled down over her long, silky hair, wanted to talk. It wasn't the time or the place. *"Auf Wiedersehen,"* I said, receiving a cute pout in return. It was time to hit the road.

As we pulled away, I wondered what she would have asked me about Elvis. I wouldn't have discussed Elvis in any case; I wasn't in the business of talking about Elvis Presley with anyone except Ira Jones.

During his first few weeks with the scout platoon, Elvis found himself doing a job that no one liked. Some idiot had decided that Headquarters Company should have the job of "sorting out brass" from the .45-caliber range at Ray Barracks, and Elvis was put on the sorting detail. There had been live-fire training on the grease gun at an old German army bunker down the hill from the main 32d Tank Battalion barracks area. The short, stocky grease gun was a low-technology, early version of the Uzi, and in those days we thought it fired pretty fast. In any case, the grease gun used up lots of .45-caliber rounds. The 3d Armored Division SOP stated that all the thousands of expended brass casings had to be checked by hand, one at a time, to be sure there were no live rounds. An officer had to supervise the job and sign a certificate stating that there were no live rounds in the piles of casings. (Of course, the officer could not possibly know with certainty that one hadn't been missed.)

The problem with Headquarters Company being given this particular job was that the grease-gun ammo had not been fired by any platoon or section of Headquarters Company, but by one of the tank company platoons! The platoon that had fired the stuff should have been given the job of sorting out its own brass, with one of its own officers signing the certificate.

I had gone down to the battalion ammunition storage area to do my required monthly inventory of B Company's spare ammo. There I found the Headquarters Company detail, including Elvis, going through the monotonous drill of taking .45-caliber brass out of boxes, inspecting it, and putting it into other boxes. They looked like a bunch of zombies going through the motions.

As I walked toward them, one of the guys called out, "Hey, Sir, how ya' doin'?"

Elvis stood up slowly from a squatting position he must have been in for a long time and stretched his limbs. He had brass casings spread out on a tank tarpaulin in front of him.

"Lootenet, you don't have to do this stuff too, do you?"

"Sure I do, every time B Company goes to one of the small-bore ranges around here."

With a frown on his face, Elvis said, "Well, D Company shot this stuff up. Why aren't they doin' this?"

"Well, everything in life isn't always fair, is it? And, by the way, D Company's priority right now is getting ready for a tank maintenance inspection. Remember that our whole reason for existence is to keep those 90mm monsters ready to move, shoot, and communicate."

"But remember, Lootenet, that those tank companies don't know where the enemy is and where to go unless us scouts tell or show 'em. We outta be workin' on our jeeps or trainin', not pickin' brass. Right?" Hell, this young guy seemed to be looking for an argument. He was still frowning.

"Presley, we need to let people senior to us, and more experienced than we are, set our priorities. That's the way the system works—and should work." Elvis studied the brass in front of him.

"To answer your earlier question a little more, let me tell you that as a private I had to do a lot of crappy jobs I didn't like much. But I did them. Like cleaning out grease traps or cleaning up someone else's piss in a latrine."

Without looking up, he said, "Lootenet, is that story about you piling shit in a sergeant's hands true?"

For crying out loud, no one ever forgets anything. Many months before, there had been an IG (inspector general) inspection of the entire battalion. Among other things, I had been responsible for making a final check of all the Headquarters

Company barracks. I had found a toilet unflushed and asked the sergeant in charge of the particular area to check it. He reported back that the toilet wouldn't flush and that he had called post support maintenance to get it fixed. I knew that the maintenance team would never get there before the IG team arrived. I tried to flush the toilet, but the water just rose in the bowl. So I pulled up my sleeve, reached deep down into the crap and toilet paper, and pulled out a handful. Then I tried the handle, and the toilet flushed properly. I looked at the sergeant (a pretty lazy guy anyway), told him to hold out his hand, and deposited the pile of crap in it. Then I told the very surprised NCO, to get it right the next time. I guess someone had been watching, or he had told the story.

"Yes, it's true."

"I'll be damned," said Elvis Presley, trying to hide a grin.

"It's all part of getting the job done—like picking brass."

"I hear ya', Lootenet," said Elvis, the grin replaced by a much too serious expression.

At that moment, my supply sergeant called, "Lieutenant Taylor, look at this." I turned away from Elvis, saying, "Be right back."

As I walked away, I heard some commotion. When I turned around, Elvis and a few other guys were throwing brass casings at each other and laughing their butts off. The boredom was broken, and I'd have bet that Elvis was the instigator. I could have reprimanded them for horseplay in the ammo area, but I couldn't bring myself to do it. Not a damn thing was dangerous about a few, small "empties" flying around the open area of the ammo dump. The guys were doing a boring job—one that should have been done by someone else—and were getting a few minutes of relief. Hell, I wasn't in charge of the detail anyway.

This incident was typical of Elvis. He always did his job and took it seriously, but he wouldn't let it wear him down. He knew how to have fun. Elvis was a master of horseplay. He was good for morale!

It didn't take too long before Elvis and I knew each other well enough for one to ask the other what we were thinking about. He always began the answer to that question with, "Hell, Lootenet, I don't know. It's just that . . ." and he would continue with whatever it was he wanted to get off his chest. He often wondered out loud about why things were the way they were. One of his questions has always stuck in my mind: "Why do people look down on other people?" Over the last two or three months we were together, this question came up twice when he was in an especially pensive mood. There must have been times when his status in life really bothered Elvis—perhaps his life in East Tupelo, Tennessee, or Memphis. I wondered who had put him down or said something to hurt him. It was hard to imagine such vulnerability now that he apparently had everything in the world going for him.

When he went into these momentary reflections, his face took on that brooding look for which he was famous—his eyes fixed on something distant, his lips impassive, his checks immobile. "Sexy looking," the women would say.

Our time together was not all serious discussion, however. There were some fun things to do to break the monotony of life in garrison at Ray Barracks. We had a small training area right outside Friedberg, where small units, such as a tank platoon or the scout platoon, could get our vehicles out for minimaneuvers. This was always more fun than sitting for hours in classrooms or putting in hundreds of hours of tedious maintenance on vehicles, engineer tools, radios, or gas masks.

Another diversion was pistol or grease-gun firing at a small range down the side of a hill near the motor pool. I knew the officer in charge, and he was happy to let me shoot there on weekends when no one else was scheduled on the range.

As a tanker, my issued weapon was a .45-caliber pistol. Elvis once said that he wished he could wear a pistol, rather than lug around his ten-pound, .30-caliber M1 rifle. He asked me where I practiced with my pistol. When I told him about the range, he asked me whether he could go with me someday.

"Lootenet, I sure would like to try my hand with your pistol. I only qualified sharpshooter with the .45."

I knew from the badges that he wore on his Class A uniform that Elvis had not achieved expert with any weapon. He had qualified sharpshooter with the M1 rifle and only marksman with the carbine in basic training at Fort Chaffee, Arkansas. That probably bothered him since many of his platoon buddies had qualified expert with at least one weapon.

"The .45 pistol is not easy to shoot with," I told him. "Beyond twenty-five meters, you can't hit a damn thing. My father was one of the best pistol shooters in the navy. He preferred to shoot a long-barreled .38 revolver. He once told me that the best use of the .45 was to run up to your enemy and hit him in the head with it."

"But it would be fun to go out and shoot the .45 with you anyway."

"Okay, we can go out on Saturday or Sunday afternoon if you want to. We can both use my pistol."

"Sure, Lootenet. Is Saturday okay? We play football on Sunday."

"Okay with me," I replied.

"What time?" asked Elvis.

"I'll pick you up at your place about 1400."

I also invited a good friend of mine, Lt. Lon Spurlock, who served with our sister battalion, the 52d Infantry. He and I practiced together often. Lon thought it would be fascinating to meet Elvis Presley. He offered to drive.

Lon picked me up shortly before two o'clock. We arrived at 14 Göethestrasse right on time, and Elvis was waiting out in his driveway, wearing his fatigue uniform and combat boots. He didn't recognize either the car or the driver, so I yelled over to him. "Any soldiers around here want to go shooting?"

"Hey, Lootenet," he said as he walked over, throwing a salute first to Lieutenant Spurlock and then a fresh one to me.

I introduced the two, then asked Elvis to take the front seat as I climbed into the back.

On the drive to Ray Barracks, we talked mainly about Graf maneuvers and the crazy incidents that had happened there. Lon didn't fawn on Elvis or ask about private things. He kept the discussion on a professional level, although his keen sense of humor kept all three of us chuckling. Elvis was interested in the differences and similarities between infantry and armor units.

"Well, Presley, the biggest problem we have in armored infantry is getting you slow-ass tankers the hell out of our way so that we close with and destroy the enemy."

"Hey, Sir, I'm not a tanker—I'm a scout. We move faster than any M59 personnel carrier. And, if it wasn't for us, nobody would know where the hell they were goin'."

"Presley," Lon needled, "infantrymen can read maps better than any scout ever born. If I took you and your friend here out in the woods and gave you a 1:2,500, you'd be lost before you got started trying to find your way home."

Elvis came right back, exclaiming, "1:2,500! Sir, that's a map so small-scale its for people who crawl. Scouts run off 1:100,000 maps, we go so fast. We roll and communicate, we don't slog around in woods."

None of this was in any way disrespectful on Elvis's part, nor did it smack of overfamiliarity. It was just plain verbal horseplay among soldiers heading out to have some fun on a weekend.

I chimed in. "Lon, you forget that I was commissioned from Infantry OCS, but was given a choice of branch and I chose armor—smartest thing I ever did." OCS stood for Officer Candidate School.

"Bullshit," snorted Lon.

As we passed through Friedberg, I quipped, "Hey Lon, do you need some scout road guards to show you how to get to the Kaserne?" Elvis laughed out loud.

"Okay, guys, okay" was Lon's reply. He knew he was out-numbered.

A few minutes later we passed through the main gate at Ray Barracks. We drove straight through, past the parade field to the 52d Infantry barracks. The old buildings had been used before World War II to house German SS units.

Lon parked outside his unit's building. "I'll be back in a couple of minutes. Do you have ammo, Bill?"

I replied that I didn't, but could get a couple of boxes when I picked up my pistol from the B Company arms room.

"Nah, I'll get some from my armorer. He's waiting for me, and I told him to have three boxes ready."

Elvis and I got out of the car too and walked over to a bench outside Lon's company headquarters. We shot the breeze about nothing in particular. Elvis sat there with his legs crossed, wriggling his foot like crazy. I remembered how often my father had told me not to do that. But for some-one with a lot of nervous energy, it's a hard habit to break. And, Lord knows, Elvis and I both had a lot of nervous en-ergy in those days. I had noticed more than once that it was difficult for Elvis Presley to sit still for any length of time. Twice when I had walked into scout platoon classes, he was standing up, leaning against a wall, while almost everyone else was seated.

I thought about repeating my father's dictum, "Don't wiggle your damn foot," but said instead, "Who do you play football with?"

"My buddies from back home—you don't know 'em. And some of the guys here in CCC. Joe Esposito's one of 'em. His barracks are right around the corner. Football's fun and good exercise."

"What position do you play?" I asked.

"Mostly quarterback."

Lon walked out carrying a cartridge belt with his .45 holster and pistol on it and boxes of ammo.

"Okay, got it. Ready?"

We got back in the car and drove down the hill to B Company, where my supply sergeant was waiting for me. I went into the supply room that also included our arms room, a section sealed off with a steel cage and kept locked to prevent theft or some drunken soldier from getting his hands on a weapon. Of course, a guy would also have to break into the ammo supply area down the road to get ammo so he could shoot a weapon. In any case, there were tight controls—losing a weapon for any reason was a cardinal sin and the cause of an official investigation.

I decided to check out two pistols so that Elvis could have his own. My supply sergeant lived in the B Company barracks, so I asked whether he or the armorer would be around at about 4:30 P.M. so I could return the pistols to the arms room. He said he would be there.

I had forgotten my holster, so I wrapped the two .45s in rags and put them in two empty .50 caliber metal ammo containers along with little cans of bore cleaner and oil, a bore brush, and bore-cleaning patches.

I returned to the car, and we drove down to the .45-caliber range. We laid out our pistols, the ammo, and all the cleaning gear on a bench. I walked over to the range equipment building, unlocked it with a key the range NCOIC had given me, and we took out three big bull's-eye targets mounted on frames and three gray cardboard silhouette targets shaped roughly like a man's upper body and head. We slipped all the targets into ground receptacles and moved back to the bench, located twenty-five yards away from the targets.

I was always a little nervous when I went on a pistol-shooting range with someone new. Lon and I had done this together plenty of times, and I knew he was safety conscious. But I had never shot with Elvis and didn't know how he would act. I got my first clue when Elvis picked up a pistol, clicked off the slide lock, snapped the receiver closed, took aim at a target, let his arm drop, then turned toward me.

I was about to say something, but Lon beat me to it. "Hey, Presley, keep that damn thing pointed downrange! When on a firing range, you must always assume that a weapon is loaded."

"Oh shit, sorry," said Elvis. He turned back toward the targets, pulled back the slide of his .45, and returned to the bench with the pistol pointed skyward.

I said, "Lon, why don't you go first."

He slipped .45-caliber rounds into his magazine, walked forward to a firing position, slammed the magazine into the receiver at the base of the handle, and released the lock so that the receiver snapped forward carrying a round into the pistol chamber. He took up a good standing position, aimed, took in a deep breath, exhaled, and slowly squeezed the trigger. Bam! His wrist jerked up. He was concentrating on nothing but the bull's-eye. Bam! Bam! Bam! Bam! Bam! Bam! He raised his pistol, released the empty magazine, pulled back and locked the slide, and walked back to the bench with his pistol aimed skyward.

Elvis was intently watching Lon's every move.

"Let's go look," said Elvis, and we walked forward to examine the target.

"Holy shit!" exclaimed Elvis. We all saw six bull's-eyes and one just outside the bull's-eye. "That is some kinda' shootin', Sir."

"Hell, Lon, you're losing your touch," I needled. "Where did that stray round come from?"

"Screw yourself, Taylor," Lon replied with a sarcastic grin.

Lon pulled a little box out of his pocket and took out some square paper patches with glue on the back. He licked the backs one at a time and pasted the squares over the holes in the target, black squares to cover the six holes in the bull's-eye and a white square to cover the other hole.

We walked back to the bench. "Go ahead, Elvis," I said.

Elvis repeated the motions Lon had gone through and took aim. Bam! The bullet hit the dirt, maybe nine or ten yards in front of the target.

"Son of a bitch?" exclaimed Elvis with a sort of questioning tone.

"Elvis, you pulled the trigger—you didn't squeeze. Pulling too fast will get you dirt every time. Line that bull's-eye up with the top of the front sight post and level with your rear sight, then breathe, take up the trigger slack, and squeeze slowly—very, very slow, steady finger pressure. You're forgetting your basic training."

"Okay, thanks, Lootenet. Here goes."

Elvis took a long time with the next shot, raising his arm, aiming, dropping his arm, and remaining steady before he squeezed off a round. Bam! No dirt spatter. That round made it. So did the next six rounds. Elvis cleared his weapon, walked back, and put it on the table. We walked out to his target. Two bull's-eyes, one in the nine circle, two in the eight circle, and two at the lower right-hand section of the target with no score. All the rounds tended to be low and to the right, even the two in the bull's-eye. I told Elvis that he needed to compensate for this just a hair; could be that his pistol was just a bit inaccurate, tending to shoot low and to the right.

I took my turn and put two in the nine circle, which brought the expected reaction from Lon Spurlock (mainly for Elvis's benefit no doubt). "Well, I'll be damned, I thought they taught pistol shooting in OCS. Guess I was wrong." Lon, as you might have guessed, was a West Point grad.

I just smiled. "Okay, let's try the silhouettes." I wasn't going to let Lon get me into any kind of competitive mood. We were both expert marksmen with the .45, but Lon was a little bit better than I, just enough to take my money most of the time when we bet. We never bet much, however, because on an army lieutenant's pay, we didn't have much.

The silhouettes were placed in a mechanism that had a long, thin steel cable running through pipes back to the firing line. A big wooden handle was hooked to the cable. When the handle was pulled, the silhouette popped up; when the handle was released, the silhouette fell back to the ground. The object was to put as many rounds as possible through the target when it was up. You never knew when the guy behind you would pull or release the handle. You had to be ready for anything.

I said, "Go ahead, Lon, I'll pull for you."

"Yeah, I'll bet you will." He figured I'd pop that target up and down so fast that he'd have a hell of a time getting one round fired at it.

You don't have time to breathe, aim, take up the slack, and squeeze at a silhouette. You have to get your sights approximately lined up and pull off your shots. You have to have a feel for how to shoot at a fast-moving silhouette. On the other hand, the silhouette of an upper body is a lot bigger than a bull's-eye, and, if you hit the silhouette anywhere, you have done terrible damage to your enemy. The .45-caliber bullet is a short, fat hunk of lead covered with copper. When it goes through a person, it punches with a terrible force, leaving a small hole where it enters and a big, ragged wound where it comes out. The force of the impact would knock a big man off his feet. It may not be played that way in movies, but that's the way it works.

Lon took up position in front of me. He preferred a pretty unorthodox position with his legs spread pretty far apart and a slight crouch, his left arm supporting his right just under his pistol grip. I pulled, the target popped up, and Lon got off two rounds before I dropped it. I pulled again, gave him some time, and he got off the five remaining rounds in quick succession. He cleared his pistol, and we went forward to look at the target. Seven shots, seven hits.

I pulled next for Elvis. He loaded his magazine and took up a karate-type stance. I pulled and left the silhouette up. He fired seven quick rounds. The result was five hits—damn good for someone who had shot the .45 only in basic training. The hits were all over the silhouette, but, again, with the .45 all you have to do is hit your enemy somewhere, and he's going down. Anyway, one of Elvis's rounds was through the head.

"Damn, Presley, that is some good shooting," said Lon.

"Sure is," I agreed.

"Thanks. This is fun!" Elvis was beaming.

I took my turn, with Lon pulling three times. I got five hits just like Elvis. All five hits were in the chest and stomach areas. Since the head area is much smaller than the chest area, I just concentrated on the critical mass—the middle of the target.

We spent more than an hour using up all three boxes of ammo. Elvis got better and better with each round of shooting. On his last turn with the silhouette, Elvis put all seven rounds into the target in four pulls. Pretty damn good, and it obviously made him feel good about himself. "Alright!" he exclaimed. "I wish I could shoot qualification again. Bet I could make expert."

"I'm sure you would. That was fine shooting," I told him.

Each of us disassembled his pistol and went through the mandatory process of careful cleaning. Elvis had forgotten how to get to the main pin that holds the receiver to the frame, so I showed him. With the cleaning and reassembly completed, we put the silhouettes in a nearby trash container, pulled off the big bull's-eye targets, and nailed new paper targets onto the frames. We picked up all the brass, then put back all the other range equipment and locked up the shed. The only smoker of the threesome, I picked up my cigarette butts, plus some others. When we left, everything looked shipshape.

We drove back to our two company areas and returned our pistols to their arms rooms. Elvis came into B Company with me, and I introduced him to my supply sergeant, who was tickled to meet him. He asked Elvis how his shooting went. Elvis paused. He was not one to brag, so I said, "He blew 'em away. Seven out of seven in his last pass at the silhouettes." Elvis just grinned and said nothing.

As we drove back through Friedberg, Lon asked if we wanted to stop for a beer. I said that I would. Elvis said, "Sure, if you want to, but can we go to a place off the main street? I know one down a back alley comin' up to the right. Too many people around here on the main street."

I knew, of course, what he meant. If someone recognized him, he would get thronged, and either he just wasn't in the mood for that, or he was being considerate of Lon and me who just wanted to sit down and have a beer. Probably the latter—Elvis seemed very sensitive about the feelings of other people.

He got us to the little Gasthaus he knew about. The alley was too narrow to park, so Lon dropped us off and took the car back up to the main street. When Elvis and I walked in, the hausfrau was sitting at one of the four small tables, reading. She recognized Elvis and said quietly with a smile, "Ooh, Herr Elvis." We shook hands and sat down. Elvis couldn't speak German, so I used the little bit of German I had learned. I ordered Elvis an orange drink and ordered *zwie bier*, explaining that another person was coming.

"Lootenet, I really appreciate you takin' me with you. Lootenet Spurlock is a nice guy. It was really a good time."

"Glad you could make it. What are you up to tonight?"

Elvis thought a second. "Well, got a girlfriend comin' over for dinner with family and friends. We'll just stay home and mess around, talk, sing some and all that—just relax. Next weekend, we're gonna travel and go to some places Esposito knows about, see some shows and stuff."

Lon walked in, greeted the hausfrau, and sat down. He thanked us for the beer and took a long, slow swig. He looked at Elvis. "Well, King of Rock, Roll, and the .45, you did fine today. Enjoyed having you with us."

Lon said to me, "It won't be long before you, Peggy, and the kids head back to the land of the big PX. Presley and I have a long time to go." Lon had been assigned to Germany long after I had, probably only a few months before Elvis arrived.

"Yeah, Peggy is ready to go home. I haven't spent a lot of time with her here. I've spent a hell of a lot of time away in the field, especially when I had the recon platoon, but even a lot with B Company."

"Where will your next assignment be?" asked Elvis.

"Don't have my orders yet, but it'll probably be your old stomping grounds at Fort Hood, Texas. Peggy would rather be on the East Coast, but I put in for another tank company command and that probably means Fort Hood."

Elvis grimaced. "Didn't like Hood much. It's a million miles from nowhere. Killeen, Texas, the nearest town, ain't much, believe me."

We went on to talk about various aspects of training, the limitations of the Friedberg training area, the problems of maneuver damage to German-owned land, and what we thought of the German people, among other subjects.

After about a half hour, Lon looked at his watch. It was getting close to six o'clock, time to go. Elvis offered to pay and insisted when Lon and I both objected—so we let him. He left a sizable deutsche mark tip for the hausfrau. She was all smiles as we left. "*Danke, danke shöen.*"

Ten minutes later, we dropped Elvis off at his home, and Lon and I headed back to our Little Texas apartments.

"Nice guy, really a nice guy. Good attitude. I like him," mused Lon, the sometime cynic, who really didn't like a hell of a lot of people.

"Yes, he is," I agreed. "I don't know a damn thing about his family life except some things Ira Jones has told me. Must not be an easy life. Jones and I both size him up to be a good soldier though, and his scout platoon buddies really like and respect him."

Lon pulled up in front of my apartment. "Lots of fun, Bill. Best to Peggy and the kids."

As I walked up to our second-floor apartment, I conjured up the smile on Elvis's face as he counted seven holes in that last silhouette. I felt good that he had felt comfortable enough to ask to go shooting with me and that the day had worked out so well. Nice guy, that King of Rock 'n' Roll.

There was one particular incident that told me a lot about how Elvis related to the members of his platoon. It happened once when I was serving "courtesy patrol" duty.

The courtesy patrol consisted of an officer (me), an NCO,

and a jeep driver. The task was to patrol the bars and streets of Friedberg that were frequented by 32d Tank Battalion soldiers on weekend passes to make sure they were observing "good order and discipline"—this meant pick up an occasional drunk and return him to his barracks, prevent or break up brawls, make sure our soldiers were wearing their uniforms properly, and generally ensure that our troops did nothing to offend our German friends.

About ten o'clock that night, I got a call on the jeep radio from our battalion duty NCO. He had received a report that one of the scout platoon guys had been sighted in Bad Nauheim in an off-limits Gasthaus known to be frequented by local whores. My task was to go find the guy and take him back to his barracks. The NCO with me knew where the Gasthaus was.

As we cranked up the jeep to go, a surprising incident happened. I saw a soldier push a girl over the hood of a car and start to slap her around. The two of them were screaming at each other. The NCO and I ran over and grabbed the guy, pinning his arms behind him. To our astonishment, the German girl started screaming at us in broken English, telling us to leave her boyfriend alone and to mind our own goddam business! I told them both to calm down, and after a few minutes they apologized to each other. The NCO and I decided to let them go.

All this must have taken about ten minutes, and then we proceeded to the Gasthaus, about ten more minutes away. When we got there, the first thing I saw was two guys getting into a white BMW sports car!

I yelled, "Presley, Lieutenant Taylor, wait a minute." Elvis opened his door, got out, and saluted with a sheepish look on his face.

"Well, Lootenet, I got a call at home sayin' one of our guys needed some help." About that time, the passenger door on Elvis's BMW opened, and someone leaned out and started puking.

"Don't mind him, Lootenet. Must have a virus or sumthin'."

"Presley, what's going on here? This place is off-limits."

"Well, Lootenet, I don't know if there's any one of our people in there. Prob'ly not, I'd say."

"Preees-ley," I began.

"Please, Lootenet, you know Frank. He's a good guy. Just made a mistake. He's got a good record. He'd help any one of us in a jam."

"Frank?" I asked.

"Well, Frank's a friend who plays football over at my place a lot. He called me sayin' that he was in this place and that there was an MP jeep outside nosin' around. He asked for help, so I came to get him. When I got here a few minutes ago the MPs were round the corner. Prob'ly still are and may come back."

"Okay," I said, "take off. I'll take care of the MPs. You want to take Frank home with you to take care of his virus, or do you want me to take him back to the barracks? If I take him in, I have to log it."

"I'll take him, Lootenet. We're gonna play football tomorrow anyway."

"How can he play football with a virus?" I asked with a sly smile.

"Well, I think some aspirin now might make him well by tomorrow afternoon," said Elvis, matching my own grin.

"Take off, Presley."

Elvis saluted. "Thanks a million." He ran to his car, cranked it up, and drove off.

The NCO on patrol with me couldn't keep the grin off his face. "Alright, Sir, alright!" he said.

We got back in our jeep and drove around the corner, and there was an MP jeep with flashing lights.

"What's up, Sergeant?" I asked as we pulled up.

"Just checkin' out a couple of whorehouses in the area, Sir."

A close call, I thought.

Elvis could have gotten himself in a jam if he had interfered with the MPs or had gone into the Gasthaus himself. Obviously, he knew that and was willing to risk an "Article 15" (nonjudicial punishment by a company commander) in order to help a buddy in his platoon. Risky, but I admired Elvis for it.

Sgt. Ira Jones and his star pupil, newly arrived Pfc. Elvis Presley near
Friedberg, Germany.

Pfc. Elvis Presley during one of his first tactical field exercises where he served as driver for Sgt. Ira Jones

Elvis receives instructions from Sgt. Jones on the proper way to live in the field during winter.

Sgt. Jones explains the platoon situation to Elvis before sending him on a mission.

Sgt. Ira Jones and Bob Hodges enjoying a beer in Bob's apartment in "Little Texas." Elvis heard many stories about Hodges's legendary exploits while a member of the Scout Platoon.

Author, 1st Lt. Bill Taylor, who became a friend and fan of Elvis Presley during their service together in Germany.

Lt. Col. Norwell Stark (with shovel) planting a tree in front of the Post Exchange at "Little Texas" where officers and noncommissioned officers lived off-post outside Bad Nauheim, Germany. On the left is Sgt. Ira Jones and Lt. Bill Taylor.

Men of the scout platoon of the 32d Tank Battalion, 3d Armored Division, the future family of Elvis Presley.

A rotten, fuzzy photo of the Scout Platoon during tactical field exercises in Germany. Elvis Presley is in the bottom row, third soldier from the right. Sgt. Ira Jones is in the top row, second from the right.

Sgt. Hodges's Jeep gets stuck in the mud. Elvis and the guys help to extract it from the goo.

Sgt. Elvis Presley examines map to check out scout platoon's future location during winter war games. *(National Archives)*

Sgt. Elvis Presley checks functioning of jeep-mounted light machine gun during war games in Germany.

Sgt. Elvis Presley briefs his reconnaissance team on a mission to check out an object many miles away during war games in Germany. Other soldiers are Pvt. Lonnie Wolfe and Spec. 4th class Hal Miller atop the jeep. (National Archives)

Elvis Presley takes aim with his rifle during scout platoon training.

Spec. 4th class Elvis Presley ready to fire the 3.5 inch rocket launcher, a deadly tank killer by 1950's standards.

Sgt. Elvis Presley checks out the terrain during winter war games in Germany.

Sgt. Elvis Presley coordinates a mutual reconnaissance mission with German soldiers.

Sgt. Elvis Presley examines Jeep for proper maintenance with fellow scout Pvt. Lonnie Wolfe.

A break in the action with Sgt. Elvis Presley finding a warm place for chow and conversation with American and German soldiers.

Sgt. Elvis Presley being interviewed by Spec. 4th class David Murdock for an Army press release, March 1, 1960. (National Archives)

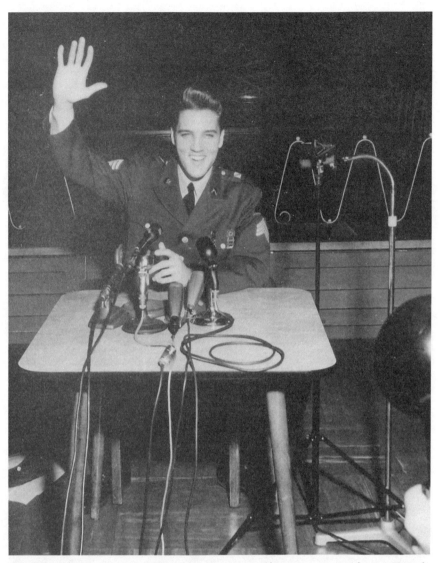

Sgt. Elvis Presley gives his last press conference in uniform. Fried-burg, Germany, March 1, 1960. (National Archives)

A happy Sgt. Elvis Presley receives his final pay and honorable discharge at Fort Dix., New Jersey, March 5, 1960.

Congratulating newly discharged Elvis Presley is Nancy Sinatra who presents him with a farewell gift at Fort Dix, New Jersey, March 5, 1960.

CHAPTER 5

ELVIS IN THE FIELD— WINTER TIME

Despite the fact that he was a darn good soldier, Elvis *hated* field training. He did his job very well when he was in the field but made no bones about his feelings. "Boy, do I hate this shit," he told me one day in the Grafenwöhr motor pool during our November–December 1958 exercise. This was Private Presley talking. He was promoted on 27 November.

We had just come back to the warmth of the Grafenwöhr cinder-block and tent city after a seventy-two-hour attack-defense maneuver out in the windblown hills of the main training area. Because this was a *graded* test of our capabilities to operate in combat (against another U.S. Army unit assigned as the aggressor force), we were "full tactical," meaning that we had to do everything the way we would do it in combat. That meant that the tops were off all jeeps and the windshields had to be in the down position with camouflage nets secured over them so they did not reflect any glare that would give away our position. Sound okay? Sure, if the season were spring, summer, or fall, but this exercise took place in the middle of a bitterly cold German winter.

Snow would have been welcomed by us all, because the weather was a slow, not-quite-freezing drizzle—wet and cold enough to chill you to the bone. This was made worse by the fact that moving jeeps created their own windchill factor. All of us who rode in open vehicles were just plain miserable. Many caught bad colds or contracted tonsillitis or pneumonia (which I developed personally on that exercise, leaving a spot on my lungs).

So there stood Elvis after seventy-two hours, saying with great seriousness and abject resignation, "Boy, do I hate this shit." We all agreed with him, but those of us who had decided to make the army a profession would take such exercises in stride because we knew field training was the best way to prepare ourselves for combat. Those who had been drafted (or those who had volunteered for the draft, knowing that their draft number would eventually come up) saw things differently. Winter maneuvers in Graf constituted one big part of the "veil of tears" to be overcome in a two-year tour of duty. I did not know until I read Priscilla Presley's book that Elvis had actually heated up a medic's thermometer to fake a fever, hoping to miss another winter field exercise! He never mentioned that to Ira Jones or me.

This particular training exercise in Graf found us all a bit more serious than usual. It was during the time of the 1958–1959 Berlin Crisis. Russian Premier Nikita Khrushchev, evidently pumped up psychologically by Soviet successes in space and their increasing arsenal of nuclear weapons, declared that the presence of American, French, and British troops in West Berlin was "a bone in the throat." He declared that we had six months to pull our troops out of West Berlin—or else. We were quite concerned about the "or else" because any major move by the Soviets against our troops in West Berlin could mean World War III. There was not a doubt that the 32d Tank Battalion would be among the first units to take on a Soviet attack and test our resolve for victory or death. The situation in November–December was really tense as we heard and read about President Eisenhower's refusal to yield to Khrushchev's threats and bluster.

Whenever we were back in the Graf barracks area, we held periodic TI&E classes to keep the troops informed. Each company had a TI&E officer responsible for preparing the classes based on information provided by 3d Armored Division Headquarters. I was the TI&E officer for B Company and took this additional duty very seriously. After all, what was said to our men influenced their thinking and their overall approach to our mission. I was determined to give them a balanced, objective view of world events. It bothered me that the information sent down by division headquarters was often better characterized as propaganda.

The word got around among the battalion officers that I was really good at TI&E and that I could get the troops to listen up. Sometimes I was asked to substitute for a lieutenant who did not like giving TI&E. As fate would have it, I was asked to give a TI&E class at Graf for Headquarters Company. This meant that many members of the scout platoon, including Elvis, attended.

I worked hard to prepare this class and to present all sides of the issue rather than the single view the information handout provided. For example, the Soviet military was characterized as a unified juggernaut that could sweep across Western Europe if so ordered. I did not downplay the seriousness of the threat and the importance of our training to be prepared to meet it, but I told the guys to think about *which* Soviet units we might face and what the situation might be for our unit. I talked about the possibility of the Berlin crisis erupting while we were in training in Graf, which was very close to the Czech border. Would we be ordered to return to Friedberg if war suddenly broke out? Would there be time? Or would our battalion be placed under the operational control of some other headquarters and committed to combat immediately against Czech units?

It was not at all clear to me if Czech forces would have the same war-fighting capabilities as Russian units, or whether they would even obey orders from Moscow. I wanted us to think about Soviet vulnerabilities and how we could exploit them, as well as Soviet strengths. The Eastern European satellite nations, after all, thought of themselves as European, not Russian. Why should we simply assume that their military units' morale in war would be high? Why just assume that they believed deeply in the communism that had been imposed on them since World War II? Would their soldiers be as motivated to defend an alien communism as we were to defend democracy? I wanted the men to look at the situation from different points of view.

I watched facial expressions to see if I was getting through, keeping them awake and thinking. Elvis and the others looked alert and pensive.

"What do you think about Czech motivation, Private Presley?"

"Don't really know, Lootenet, but even if they don't like communism, they may fight hard because the Russians will make 'em do it. But I'd rather fight for somethin' like what America stands for."

I went on to talk about Soviet equipment. Did anyone really believe that their T54 and T55 tanks could stand up to our M48, 90mm gun tanks? And we had the new, even better, M60 model tanks coming into our inventory. Sergeant Callender raised his hand. A tanker before coming to the scout platoon, he told us a few things he had heard about the new M60.

I wanted our guys to think about ways to use our superiority in tank technology to get multiple Soviet kills in tank unit engagements. I wanted all of them to know that superior training, combined with superior equipment, was a "force multiplier" that could enable us to take on much bigger tank units and beat the hell out of them. I wanted all of them—down to every private—to understand what the prevailing U.S. doctrine of the times, mobile defense, was all about. I emphasized the *offensive* aspects of our low-level unit involvement in a very big 3d Armored Division mobile defense. I pounded home the historically proven idea that an attacker needed a three-to-one numerical advantage to overcome a well-planned defense and emphasized that an attacker in the open was vulnerable to small-unit counterattacks. I stressed one main theme: "We are an armor unit; our comparative advantages are in our mobility, firepower, and shock action."

Although the specter of Soviet battlefield tactical nuclear and chemical weapons worried me as much as anyone, I wanted our soldiers to know that there were measures we could take to defend against them, and that if the Soviets were crazy enough to use them against us, we had our own capabilities to retaliate in kind and even to escalate to more powerful nuclear weapons.

A lot of this sounds as if it might have gone over the heads of these men. Many in the room didn't even have a high school education. But I firmly believed that taught patiently in understandable language, using familiar analogies, all these ideas could be brought home to anyone. I stopped periodically and asked questions to make sure I was getting through to everybody.

I went into my summary: "If we go to war against larger Soviet forces, we can win. We can win because our allies in democracy will stick with us. We can win because our cause is right, because our equipment is better, because the 32d Tank Battalion is better trained than any tank unit the Soviets have, because we can outthink and outmaneuver them, and because victory or death is no choice at all!"

My aim was to motivate as well as inform. It worked; the guys started clapping. No one ever applauded a training class, so that felt good—mission accomplished. But that wasn't the end. Elvis and a few of the guys walked up front to talk.

"Shit, Sir," said one of the scout platoon guys, "that was great. I mean it. But you've been talking about tanks. What if the scout platoon runs across Soviet tanks?"

"Well, if our intelligence is good enough, you won't. But if you do, you get on the radio, report the location, direction, and rate of travel of those tanks, and get the hell out of there."

"Run?"

"Call it anything you want. Scouts don't fight enemy armor units. In fact, scouts are not paid to fight anything they can possibly avoid. The battalion needs more than anything else the eyes and ears that scouts provide."

"What about us in the mortar platoon?" asked another guy.

"You're our close-in fire support. For example, if my B Company is about to move into the attack, you can fire smoke rounds between us and the enemy to blind him. And you can help pound his ass to make him keep his head down as we race across open terrain to engage him. We'll be asking for artillery and air support too, but you guys are the battalion's most immediate, most responsive, best overhead fire support."

Elvis listened attentively, taking it all in.

After that session B Company went out for more field training, and I did not see Elvis for a few more days. When we got back, I went to the Graf motor pool. There was Elvis at the wash rack using a high-pressure hose to wash off the thick mud and gravel that had caked on his jeep. We waved, and I shot the breeze with my own jeep driver for a while. When Elvis finished his job, he parked the jeep and walked over.

"How's it goin', Lootenet?"

"Well, not bad, if you enjoy spending the best part of a day trying to get a tank out of the mud."

"Tell me about it?"

I began the story. The day before had really been a pain in the ass. B Company had conducted an attack on an objective out in the main training area. In my briefing to the platoon leaders before we began, I had warned the third platoon leader, who would be on the right flank in the attack, that he would be moving across low ground that would probably be muddy as hell, given all the spring rain, and that he had to be careful to skirt any dips in the terrain.

Elvis chimed in, "Hell, Sir, I'll bet it was Lieutenant ——— [name withheld]. They say that guy can't pour piss out of a boot."

I didn't say who it was but went on to describe how the third platoon got two of its tanks bogged down in deep mud. One of the two tank commanders was smart enough to know he was stuck, so he had his driver shut down the engine and waited until I brought up the company VTR (vehicle tank recovery, used for pulling or winching out stuck tanks, changing tank engines, and other such purposes in the field). The other tank commander figured he could drive his tank out of the mud. He had his driver rev the engine in forward and reverse, trying to "rock" it out of the mud, like you might do in a car. But his combat-loaded, fifty-ton tank just dug in deeper and deeper until nothing but the turret, gun, and upper deck was above ground level.

I called up our VTR and had it hook the winch cable to the rear of the stuck tank and try to slowly pull it out of the mud. The tank hardly moved, and I was getting nervous about the winch cable snapping. When a heavy steel cable snaps under great pressure it becomes a lethal, unpredictable weapon; it could lash out in any direction and could cut a man in half. So I stopped that operation.

"Yeah, I know what you mean," Elvis said. "A construction guy told me about that once."

I continued the story. My maintenance sergeant, a terrific NCO with many years of experience, came up with the idea of hooking several of our tanks together by their towing cables, like Santa Claus's reindeer, and using all the engine power and the ground traction of multiple treads to pull out our stuck behemoth. The stuck tank also used its own engine and track power at a low rpm. At first there was only a slow inching forward; then all the combined power came together at the right moment. The big beast surged forward and shook loose from the pressure and suction of the mud. Everyone started cheering as if we had freed a horse from quicksand.

Elvis listened to this description pretty intently. "Yeah, we got some damn good NCOs in the 3d. Yeah, makes sense. I'll remember that."

"You know, Presley, the thing that bothered me about the whole deal was that B Company had two tanks out of action, one of them for hours. That's a lot of lost combat power, which could cost us dearly in a real war. And it was unnecessary. The two tank commanders could have found higher, dryer ground only a couple hundred yards to their right. That kind of mistake costs lives."

"Sergeant Jones gave me a little hell for sticking three-one a few days ago."

"What happened?" I asked.

"Well, we were movin' pretty fast from one piece of high ground to another place where we could get better observation on the aggressor and could communicate and report better."

I could picture what he was talking about. In those days, most of our radios were pretty bad, with short, line-of-sight communications. If your vehicle wasn't on high ground communicating to another radio also on high ground, you couldn't hear much. Nowadays, vehicle radios relay their signals via satellite over great distances.

"Sergeant Jones was looking at his map and tryin' to talk on the radio. I got off the road to take a shortcut to an intersection and jumped three-one right into an area that musta' had a spring under it. Jones had to call a scout section to come pull us out."

I grimaced.

"You ever seen Sergeant Jones when somethin' like that happens? You ever seen that look on his face?"

I knew exactly what Elvis meant. Jones would seldom get mad or raise his voice. More often he would just say, "Well, God damn, soldier, ain't we taught you better than that?" The comment was normally accompanied by Jones pulling his six-foot-four-inch frame to full height and standing with his hands on his hips. Pretty intimidating, even though the soldier on the receiving end never doubted Ira Jones's loyalty and friendship. When Jones expressed disappointment in someone's lack of training or tactical judgment, it was like letting down your father. Even as Jones's commanding officer, I would have been devastated if he had ever shown disappointment in me, in any way.

"Well, you woulda' thought I had lost a war or somethin'," Elvis said. "He told me that little mistakes like that were mistakes we wanted the Soviets to make, not us."

"Have a seat," I said, motioning to a nearby concrete grease rack. "You know, we all make mistakes. The trick is to make them in training and learn how to correct them before we ever get into the real thing with the Soviets."

Elvis looked pensive.

"Even in combat, the best leaders make mistakes, but you can't afford to make big ones, or too many little ones. Talking about winning on the battlefield, Napoleon once said, 'It's not he who makes no mistakes, but he who makes the fewest mistakes.'"

"Yeah, we all make some mistakes, no matter what we do or how hard we try not to. Lord knows I wish I could go back and change some things," said Elvis, looking down at the muddy ground.

Elvis was sitting with his arms out straight next to his thighs, balancing on the edge of the concrete ramp, his feet not touching the ground. As he talked he was swinging his legs back and forth like a little boy. He had a mournful look on his face and he spoke slowly and softly. "You know, if I hadn't been on the road so much, I could've taken care of my family better. Spent too much time thinkin' about myself."

I sat there thinking about Elvis's dependents at 14 Göethestrasse, and I wondered what in hell he could be doing to take better care of his family. I also thought about my own family. Since I enlisted in the army, I had spent a lot of time away from Peggy and our growing family, not to mention my parents.

"Me too. There's just not enough time to do everything and touch all the bases at the right time. My dad's not well, and I worry about him. He's living in a big house all alone now. He's got diabetes and he drinks too much. But here I am in

Germany for three years. I can't afford to fly home to see him, and even if I could, I need to spend more time than I do now with my wife and children. And if I went home, I'd also have to spend time with my mother and stepfather and my wife's parents. There wouldn't be enough time to do it all."

Elvis didn't say anything for a minute or two. Then, "Well, I could have done a lot more for my momma." He slid off the ramp to stand in the mud. Big, heavy rubber galoshes covered his leather combat boots.

I decided not to touch that comment. It sounded like a very sad past tense—I knew nothing about the circumstances and he didn't elaborate. It looked as if Elvis was finished sitting and talking anyway.

But Elvis wasn't finished talking. He leaned against the ramp and looked at me.

"Is it right about your middle name bein' Jesse, Lootenet?"

"Now, Presley, let's not get into that." I reflected on the number of times that kids at school had teased me about my middle name. They'd say "Jesseee" or "Hey, Jess" to see if they could get a rise out of me. Actually, I didn't mind the name, only the way some guys would try to play on it for fun.

"Whadaya' mean? Jesse's a fine name. You got any brothers or sisters, Lootenet?"

"Nope, just me. How about you?"

"Well, I did have a little brother—an identical twin, Momma said—but the Lord took him away from me right from the start. His middle name is Jesse too." I noticed that Elvis said "is."

"Spelled how?" I asked. "With an *e* or an *ie*? Mine's with just an *e*."

"My daddy's daddy's middle name was with an *ie*, but my brother's name is the same as yours."

"You know, I've never met another guy with the name, but it goes pretty far back in my family. I'm William J. Taylor Jr. only because in my family, when a William Jesse dies, his son's name is moved up a number. I was born William Jesse III, but when my father's father died, I became Jr. and my dad dropped the Jr. from his name. I don't know why we did this, but it didn't matter much to me. My son has the nickname Tod just because my wife liked it, but his real name is William Jesse Taylor III. I hope he keeps it that way for the rest of his life."

Elvis pondered, "I wonder if I'll ever have a son. Maybe I'll name him Jesse after my brother."

"What happened to your brother?"

"Oh, I mean he just never made it. He was my twin at birth, but I made it and he didn't. Sad, real sad, for Momma. For me too when I think about it. I always wonder why. We woulda' been best friends."

"I understand. I have wished often that I had a brother or sister, but my mother almost died from loss of blood when I was born, and my parents were afraid to try again."

I chuckled, partly to break the surprising sadness of the moment as Elvis reflected on the brother he still spoke of in the present tense, saying, "Besides, my parents could not have handled another one like me."

It crossed my mind that it was just as well that there had been no brother or sister to share my sadness at ages seven to nine, when my parents were separated, then divorced. I wondered at that moment whether there would have been two Kings of Rock 'n' Roll had Jesse Presley lived.

Elvis just gave a resigned sort of smile and exhaled. "Yeah. Well, Lootenet, it's funny about you and my brother both bein' Jesses. Good name—yeah, good name. I like it."

Elvis switched the subject.

"You know, Lootenet, I learned a lot from your talk the other day. Anything new happen?"

"Probably nothing will happen. Eisenhower isn't the kind of guy who scares easily. You remember that he's the guy who commanded our forces—heck, all allied forces—at the Normandy landing in World War II and led them all across Europe until the Germans realized that we were cleaning their clocks and surrendered. We're not leaving Berlin."

"Thanks, Lootenet," Elvis said. His grin was back. I jumped down off the ramp, and we both started walking to our jeeps, knowing we had things to get done.

"Don't get stuck in the mud," I yelled back.

As a company executive officer, I could not leave the wash racks for a couple more hours. It took a long time for the seventeen tanks and other vehicles of B Company to line up at the wash bays where we used pressure hoses to pry loose literally tons of thick mud and rock that had accumulated over three days of maneuvers.

When I finally got back to the cinder-block barracks, into which about twenty other lieutenants and I were jammed with folding canvas cots, there was a message waiting for me. The new Combat Command commander had volunteered me to accompany two French generals who were visiting Graf to observe U.S. Army training the next morning. Our headquarters back in Friedberg had screened officer personnel records to find someone who could speak French, and someone saw that I had studied French for ten years. Of course, I did not know French military jargon or the French words for various types of weapons or tactics. But the message didn't ask whether I wanted this assignment, or if I thought I could pull it off, it just told me where to report at nine o'clock to serve as translator.

I woke up at my normal 4:30 A.M. time, apprehensive as hell about the day's mission, and lay on my cot thinking out French conversational phrases and wondering what the French words for "Browning automatic rifle" or "line of departure" might be. I showered and shaved, cleaned my web gear with a brush, put a final spit shine on my boots, and went over to the B Company mess building for some coffee and to meet up with my driver.

We took off at about 7:30 A.M., winding our way down the dirt roads between the cinder-block barracks, heading out to the training area map coordinates I had been given. As we rounded a turn near the Headquarters Company motor pool area, there came HQ31 with Elvis driving Ira Jones. They saw the "B6" on my jeep's bumper, and we both pulled off to the opposite sides of the road. No reason to stop, but we did.

"Mornin', Sir. Mornin', Mac," said Sergeant Jones, returning our salutes.

It never mattered which one of us saluted first. Most people thought that enlisted men always saluted officers first, but I had been taught in OCS that a salute was not a sign of subordination, but an exchange of respect among professional soldiers. Actually, the salute developed from the ancient custom of knights in armor holding up their right hands to show each other that they were not holding weapons and came in peace.

"Good morning, Sergeant Jones, Presley. How's it going? Where are you headed?"

"Got to check out one of the areas where we're going to do aggressor duty over the next few days. Been pretty wet out there. Got to know the terrain."

"Yes, and of course, you don't want three-one up to the antenna in mud, do you?" I said, looking at Elvis.

"Now, Lootenet, you know better'n that. Scouts don't get stuck like some tankers." There was that friendly competitiveness again—and that devilish smile.

We shot the breeze about some things going on during the next few days and when we would be heading back to Friedberg and our families.

"What you up to today, Sir?" asked Ira Jones.

I told him about my mission and my concerns.

"Well, better you than me. Glad I don't have to do it. You'll think of something."

Elvis piped up, "How ya' know the French guys don't speak some English?"

"You think I could be so lucky?" I replied.

"Hell, Lootenet, you got nuthin' but luck. You're about the luckiest guy I know around here." Jones smiled at me, but Elvis was dead serious.

"Well, we'll see. Have a good recon." We all saluted casually, got back in our jeeps, and took off.

What a miserable day it was! I didn't know the French words for tank, 90mm gun, machine gun, artillery, retrograde movement, or *any* of the military terminology. I tried my very best, and at the end of the day the two French generals (who sensed my anguish) thanked me profusely. No such support from the ranking U.S. officer, however. "Lieutenant, you don't speak French very well, do you?" the colonel said to me right in front of the two foreign generals. I doubled my resolve never to criticize a subordinate in public, especially without knowing the circumstances.

That night, I was really down. My friend and former company commander, Capt. Jack Cochran, listened to my sad story and suggested that we leave the barracks area and drive into the little town of Grafenwöhr for a "sightseeing tour." We both knew that this was against regs but decided to chance it for a few mugs of the famous local beer. Known affectionately as "Captain Jack," Cochran was a short, stocky guy who knew all the human dimensions of soldiering. He decided that I needed a shot of morale and that he was the guy to provide it.

Forget the details about how we got the jeep off post, but soon I was driving jeep B6 under my old friend's guidance. He knew the most hidden route. Obviously, this was not his first foray into town. Jack Cochran was a pro at almost everything, and when he was breaking regulations, he was as sly as a fox. We drove to the outskirts of the town, looking for a very discreet Gasthaus Cochran said he had "heard about." He found it with ease, and we drove up to the large, wooden front gate. Cochran dismounted and quickly unlatched the gate so we could drive into the cobblestone courtyard. It was pretty obvious that Captain Jack had been here before.

There were two other jeeps in the courtyard. And one of them was HQ31! Seeing the scout platoon jeep there brought back fond memories of my time with the platoon. I could see that the "Hodges's tradition" was still part of the soul of the scout platoon and that Elvis had been well indoctrinated.

I parked in front. Cochran unscrewed the radio antenna and laid it across the backseat. "Antennas sticking up over the gate are telltales for the MPs," he explained.

As we walked inside, I chuckled, remembering Sergeant Hodges and his antics. Ira Jones and I had let Hodges do many of the wild things for which he became famous; he was so damn good at his job that we just looked the other way. One of them was a routine that occurred on many of our independent route reconnaissance training missions. We would leave the Kaserne early, before reveille, do our route or area recon missions all day, and stop at a Gasthaus on the way "home."

I couldn't recall how many times the old recon platoon went to a Gasthaus, but I surely remembered the routine: A radio call from Hodges, who normally had the lead in movement, to Ira Jones or me; the message—"Assemble as planned at Checkpoint Fourteen." (He had devised a code—each Gasthaus was a numbered checkpoint.) The entire platoon would monitor their vehicle radios, so everyone knew where to go.

Elvis later told me that the routine as established by Hodges had not changed. One of the NCOs would have the courtyard gates open when the platoon got there. They'd roll in, dismount, close the big courtyard gates, and take down their telltale antennas (which in everyday operations carried yellow, triangular Cavalry pennants). One member of the platoon would remain in the courtyard to monitor the platoon radio in case a call came in from company or battalion headquarters. In the Gasthaus, the hausfrau, husband, and older children—who knew the men well—would bring in large, cool (not cold) local draft beers and some wonderful kinds of *Wurst* and *Bröchen* (delicious German rolls). It was hardly debauchery. The men would normally have one big beer, eat, joke, and laugh a lot, then leave to continue the road march back to the Kaserne.

This was the independent, free-spirited platoon that Elvis was now part of. The scout platoon dared to risk a few things (such as violating minor regulations) if it served the interests of unit morale and cohesion. Napoleon once said, "Morale makes up three-quarters of the game." The Gasthaus stopovers sure as hell had helped our platoon's morale.

When Cochran and I walked into the Gasthaus, sure enough, there was Elvis; Sgt. Billy Wilson, a very competent scout section leader; and two other scout platoon soldiers I had seen before but didn't know because they joined the platoon after I left it.

I walked over to their table, saying, "My fellow Americans, my eyesight is so poor that I do not recognize you."

Wilson stood up and started waving his arms in front of his face. "I have smoke in my eyes and can't tell who you are."

Elvis stood up too, taking an unlit cigarillo out of his mouth. "Yeah, it's smoky in here. And it's so foggy outside that I don't even know where we are! How ya' doin', Sir," he said to Captain Cochran. "Lootenet," he said, smiling at me.

We laughed at the deception plan, and Cochran and I moved to the opposite side of the Gasthaus so as not to interfere with their party. We all had one hell of a fine time.

Jack Cochran and I talked for maybe an hour over three or four small beers. Mainly, I asked him questions about the "Old Army." A veteran sergeant from the Korean War, he was full of stories about small-unit combat, administration, operations, and logistics—what worked and what failed, and the consequences of poor planning and stupid decisions.

Cochran could switch from the superserious to the hilarious, telling some of the funniest stories about life in the military I have ever heard. He was so self-confident, that he told jokes on himself about mistakes he had made. And each one taught me something. I was suddenly feeling much better—and that was Captain Cochran's reason for taking me out.

"I've got to take a leak," I finally said.

"Well, your bladder grows with age and practice," he quipped with a chuckle, as he ordered another round of beers. "Damn, it's smoky in here. I thought you were quitting that habit," he said.

"I did. I hated quitting, so I stopped," I said, lighting up one more before I got up from the table. "Where's the latrine?"

"Out the front door. Go left around the pile of shit and it's there."

"The pile of shit" was the big mound of cow manure common in many Gasthaus courtyards. Most villages raised their own cattle, pigs, and geese and grew their own vegetables. The manure was very valuable fertilizer, and they piled it inside the courtyards for both security and convenience. The first time you saw it was a surprise, and the smell was rather unusual next to a restaurant. But you got accustomed to it.

So out I went, turned left around the manure pile, and saw a side door. I opened the door and inhaled the strong smell of urine. I waited for the guy at the urinal (a slanted trough running out through the wall) to finish. He heard the door, looked around, and said, "Oh, hi, Lootenet." It was Elvis.

"How you doing? It stinks in here."

"No more than our place," he said, referring, I guessed, to the latrine in his Graf barracks.

He finished and walked out. There was no running water. I remembered one of those old army sayings: "You don't have to wash your hands if you don't piss on them."

I relieved myself (making sure that I didn't), zipped up, and started walking around the manure pile, when I heard, "How's it goin', Lootenet?" Elvis had waited for me.

"Not worth a damn until tonight, my friend," I answered.

"What's wrong?" asked Elvis.

I had a passing thought that it was not proper for a lieutenant to tell an enlisted man that he had any problem at all. But my way had always been to let my guys know that we were in this thing together. Admit your mistakes and your problems. Let your team help you. Let them know that it's okay to admit they don't know something. Teams are not built on self-promoting, defensive "bullshit," but on individual members reinforcing each other. Isn't that what Jack Cochran was doing for me tonight?

Elvis said, "Cowshit doesn't smell bad when you get used to it. Wanna talk, Lootenet?"

I decided to do just that. Maybe I could pass on a lesson to or learn something from a soldier who cared. The fact that Elvis wanted to talk about my day, even after I had warned him that it was not worth a damn, sheds some important light on who Elvis Presley was at age twenty-four. Always the center of attention, he could have developed an enormous ego. Yet, what I saw was a guy who cared a lot about other people. I liked that a lot.

"Well, I was ordered to do something I couldn't do very well, and I *didn't* do it very well," I told him.

"What?" He seemed surprised.

"Remember the French generals?" I went through the story in shorthand, being very careful not to criticize the colonel. To criticize a senior officer in front of a subordinate would have been unforgivable. (And, as I had discovered that day, it wasn't much fun to be on the receiving end of criticism.)

"Well, Lootenet, you did your best. You can't blame yourself."

"Yes, I can. The second I got the order, I should have said something to the effect that I wasn't prepared to converse in French on military affairs."

"Why didn't you say so?"

"I got the order late after we cleaned up the tanks, maybe 2000 or 2100 hours. I wouldn't have been able to contact the right staff officers. They wouldn't have had time to find someone else. Hell, there isn't anyone else who could have done the job. I *had* to do it, even though I knew it would be a big-ass problem for me. What else could I do? Say no? Not show up? I did it, but I sure didn't like it."

"Yeah, know what you mean. So you did your best."

We stood in silence for a few seconds, while I field-stripped my cigarette (knock off the burning end, stomp on it, rip the paper into a tiny ball, and heave it).

Elvis gazed down at the ground, then looked up and said, "Shit, we all go through things like that. Me too. I do the best I can. Somehow it's never good enough for somebody. Sometimes I feel like just quittin'. Screw 'em all. But, can't do that. Too many people dependin' on me. Too many people think I'm goin' places. Too damn many people!"

That conversation by the manure pile was my deepest entry into Elvis's thinking. He had a whole lot on his mind and a lot more on his shoulders. It's revealing that he didn't talk about what *he* wanted: he talked about the others who depended on him and what *they* wanted and expected of him.

I've discovered through the years that the mark of success is, first and foremost, understanding where you want to go and why. Elvis sounded as if others were driving him toward goals and objectives without his deciding whether these goals and objectives were the right ones for him, and whether he would know how to get there.

Hearing Elvis bare his soul made me stop thinking about myself. I felt weak for telling this fine young man about my insignificant problem.

"My friend, *you* are doing damn well," I told him. "You are a big part of the scout platoon team. Sergeant Jones says so. I'm sure Captain Betts thinks so. You ought to be feeling good about yourself."

"Lootenet, you don't need to feel down about today. You're the best damn officer in this battalion. Everybody knows it. I—"

I cut him short, but I did not miss what he said. Maybe he knew that I needed a "buck up." Maybe not. But that statement, at that time, in that setting, meant a great deal to me. It was more important to me than any army award or decoration.

"Thanks, friend," I said. "Today's over. I learned some lessons. We all have to learn something every day."

"You're right, Lootenet. You know, when we're out in the field, we learn stuff that really can't be taught in classes. Or the stuff from classes all of a sudden means something. Well, I don't know. But I guess this Graf shit helps us."

I picked up on the "us." He didn't say "helps *me*." Elvis thought in terms of his team. I sensed that he wasn't finished talking, so I lit another cigarette.

"What are you going to do when you get out?" I asked.

"For sure, back to the grind."

I thought, the "Elvis the pelvis" grind, but I asked him a straight question: "What grind?"

"Well, Lootenet, you are in charge of your life. I'm not. Got people pushin' me. Got people givin' me advice. I got too damn much."

I dragged on my cigarette.

"Got a light?" Elvis asked.

I lighted the cigarillo he had been sucking on. It took a long time to light up. I noticed the smell of cowshit again. "Smells great out here."

"Not too bad. Whadaya' gonna do tomorrow?"

"B Company has two days to get ready for a tank company attack exercise."

"Who's the aggressor?" Elvis asked.

"Maybe you guys," I answered.

Elvis got an interested look on his face. "We're pretty good at aggressor duty. You can't keep us out—or so you said."

"My friend, you would pay hell trying to get through B Company's security perimeter. We would anticipate every move you might make."

"Yeah, maybe. But are you sure?"

Of course, he knew the answer. I had always told the recon platoon that there was no such thing as a defense perimeter that couldn't be penetrated at night by a well-trained, patient aggressor.

What could I say? My answer was, "Yes, I know what you mean. But you guys would not be able to penetrate B Company's perimeter. Everything you and Jones know, I know. Everything we have learned together, I have taught, or am teaching, my B Company guys."

"Well, Lootenet, we thirty-nine guys already know what you're *trying* to teach your hundred and twenty guys." A big grin.

All I could say was, "Okay, we'll see."

The Gasthaus door opened at that point and Cochran walked out.

"Smells great out here. You two got the world's problems solved?"

He walked past us and around the manure pile. Captain Cochran walked with the apparent determination of a banty rooster—even when he was heading for the latrine.

"Everybody likes him a lot, don't they," said Elvis.

"Yes, and he's the best company commander I ever had. He's been around the army a long time. He really cares about his people, and they all know it. I would do almost anything for him."

"Sergeant Jones is like that too."

"He sure is, Presley, he sure as hell is."

Clearly, Ira Jones had become a father figure for Elvis, just as he had for so many of the young soldiers in his charge over the years.

The latrine door slammed and Cochran emerged from the shadows. "By my calculations, the MPs ought to be making their rounds to this place in a half hour or so."

I hadn't thought about that. Depending on who the MPs were, we could get written up for being AWOL (absent without leave). And it wouldn't be a good thing for our names to appear the next day on the military police blotter for the provost marshal to see and report to our battalion commander.

"Hey, Sir, the lootenet doesn't think the scouts can get through his company's security."

Captain Cochran chuckled. "Well, we might see in a couple of days."

As the battalion S4 (supply officer), Cochran knew all our training plans because he was responsible for making sure all the fuel, lubricants, spare parts, blank ammo, food, water, and the whole mountain of supplies tank units consumed were delivered to the right place, at the right time, and in the right quantities. He had a schedule for every unit's activities.

"Hey, Sir, I gotta complaint about the chow," Elvis said to Cochran.

"What the hell's wrong with the chow? It's standard GI issue, the world's best chow for the world's best soldiers," replied Cochran with a big grin on his face.

Elvis was smiling. "Well, there isn't enough peanut butter in those little C ration cans, and when we get hot chow, the cooks serve up limp bacon. Can't make decent sandwiches."

"Private Presley, I don't manufacture C rations or cook bacon, I just deliver the stuff, then it's up to you. Do what Lieutenant Taylor does—trade." He took off his cap and rubbed his stubby left hand over his crew cut, slightly graying hair.

"Sir, don't start that. Please," I said, shaking my head. He was referring to a technique I had learned long ago from none other than the notorious Sgt. Bob Hodges, an expert in how to beat the system. When I first arrived in Germany, Hodges had told me that local German farmers were always ready to trade fresh sausages, eggs, and those great German rolls for our high-calorie garbage or even C rations, which they would feed to their pigs. With rare exceptions, such as full tactical training exercises when you couldn't light fires to cook, my troops ate good fresh German food. Sometimes I could even get a farmer to throw in a few bottles of local brew.

I didn't want too many people to know about this because trading was against regulations. But the good food sure was a big morale builder. And the regs were stupid in this case—as in many cases. I suppose there was concern at higher headquarters about risk of sickness, since German farmers used raw manure to fertilize their fields and were not very antiseptic in their methods of preparing vegetables. But German farm families always looked pretty healthy to me! I do not know of a single case where one of my soldiers got sick from eating the local food I obtained.

Cochran took great delight in telling Elvis the whole story.

"Well, there's still not enough peanut butter in those field rations," said Elvis, ragging Cochran but in a joking but respectful manner.

I heard sometime later that the day after our Gasthaus escapade a two-and-a-half-ton supply truck pulled up in front of the scout platoon barracks and delivered a whole case of peanut butter to the platoon. When asked by a scout why the case was being delivered, the truck driver replied that it beat the hell out of him, but the S4 had just said to do it. Typical Jack. That delivery was clearly against regs, but I'll bet it had a big impact on Elvis. It showed how a professional officer cares about his troops. (It never would have crossed Cochran's mind to expect anything in return.)

Cochran put his cap back on and the three of us walked back into the Gasthaus. Cochran said in a voice just loud enough for Sergeant Wilson to hear, "Well, anyone from the 32d who might be in here better think about moving it before the next patrol comes by. Normally happens about midnight."

"See you, Sirs," said Elvis with a smile as he headed back to his table. Wilson was looking a bit wobbly; it was a good thing that Elvis didn't drink and could drive the jeep.

Then Elvis turned back to me. He couldn't resist one parting shot. "Maybe I'll see you inside your perimeter, Lootenet."

"*Sure* you will. When rabbits grow horns!"

As Cochran and I walked out, the hausfrau and her husband came to say good-bye. Jack received a big handshake from the husband and a big hug from the wife. All this at the Gasthaus Cochran had just "heard about."

Out we went, past the manure pile in the courtyard. I got the antenna out and screwed it back into the mount. Cochran got in and said, "Home, Jeeves."

I opened the big wooden gate, cranked up B6, and backed it out. I closed and latched the gate, and we drove off.

"Take a right into that alley," said Cochran, "and shut off the lights." I did. A vehicle on the main road passed by the alley.

"It's the MPs. Wait for a minute." I waited till he gave me the go-ahead.

"How did you know it was the MPs and not a German car?"

"On cobblestone roads like this, you just look at the headlights coming at you. If they tend to bump up and down fast, it's a jeep on hard springs and hard shocks. If the headlights sort of roll up and down, it's a civilian vehicle on soft springs and shocks."

Once again, I thought about how much this guy had been around. You could learn a lot from an old pro!

When we got back to our barracks area, I dropped off Captain Cochran, drove B6 into the motor pool, and walked back to my barracks. I looked at my watch—almost 1:30 A.M., and I had to be up early to brief B Company on our attack exercise. Fortunately, in those young days, I didn't need much sleep.

I went to bed that night thinking about Elvis's challenge and how I would keep those scouts from penetrating our tank company's night security perimeter. Presley was right. I would pay hell trying to get our company up to the scout platoon's skill level. There was so much left to teach the guys in B Company. The company commander focused on maintenance—crucial for a tank company. As the executive officer, I naturally supported this priority, but was also trying to get our platoon leaders and platoon sergeants to focus on the importance of tactical operations. This tension was constant between staying prepared for constant inspections by higher headquarters on maintenance and record keeping, and being tactically proficient for combat.

I recalled a simple question that Elvis had asked me in one of our discussions back at Ray Barracks. "Lootenet, do we want to *look* good on paper, or *be* good on the ground?" A perceptive question for a young soldier without much military experience.

The answer for any decent army leader was difficult to give. The easy answer was that the question was framed incorrectly. The question wasn't either/or. The issue was whether a unit could be good at both, simultaneously, all the time. But I was not about to give Elvis—or any other soldier—that kind of easy answer.

I'd told him that if I had to make the choice, it would always be to keep our killing systems running, no matter what they *look* like. Good-looking paint on a tank won't stop Soviet tank rounds. The enemy doesn't give a damn whether our boots are shined or whether we're shaven. The enemy cares whether we can shoot straight and maneuver well.

This is what I had driven home to the recon platoon and was trying to convey to B Company. My priorities were know your stuff; keep your killing systems in top shape, and be able to move, shoot, and communicate better than any other unit in the world; support each other, because you absolutely need each other; and appearances count little in combat. If we ever went up against Ira Jones and his crew, I'd get the chance to see how much B Company had learned.

The next morning while I was showering, I reflected on breaking regs—which is what we'd all done last night. How can a soldier break military regulations and still be considered a good soldier? If you haven't served in the military, you just wouldn't know. Some rules you never break; some you do. If I was asked outright whether I had been into Graf, I would be honor bound to say yes. But I knew I wouldn't be asked. I felt confident that Wilson and Elvis wouldn't be asked either. And it was not something any of us would talk about or brag about.

The subject came up only once more between Elvis and me. We had another chance meeting in the motor pool, and I asked him how he felt about Graf. He replied, smiling, "Well, Lootenet, Graf is only 99.9 percent a pile of crap, especially if you get lost in the fog once in a while—if you know what I mean." I did know.

CHAPTER 6

ELVIS BACK IN GARRISON

Back in Friedberg, Elvis and I saw each other every day or so in the motor pool, walking down the battalion main street, in the PX, or somewhere else over the next few weeks. It always impressed me that Elvis looked meticulous whether in or out of uniform. Only the platoon's Sergeant Gibson looked as sharp as Elvis. In fact, Ira Jones told me that Elvis and Gibson had a daily contest on spit shines.

Our paths crossed one Saturday afternoon at the PX in Little Texas. I was shopping with my very pregnant wife, my daughter, and my little son in a baby stroller when Elvis came up behind us. I was surprised that he would go to the PX and take the chance of being mobbed by fans.

"Hi Lootenet, Mrs. Taylor. Hey, Jill."

He leaned down to look at Tod. "Hey little fella', now what's your name?"

He chucked Tod under the chin and tousled his hair. That Elvis smile could work its charm on people of all ages, but this was the first time I had seen Elvis around a baby. He took his cap with the 32d Tank Battalion crest pinned to the front and put it on Tod's head. He was rewarded with a big, two-front-teeth grin and squeal of delight. Elvis's eyes lit up. He patiently retrieved his hat—which Tod was now clutching and chewing—and turned to Jill, as if to make sure she had her share of attention. Jill had no idea who Elvis was. She was only five and a half years old. Elvis's records were being played on the radio, but only the American and German teenagers were discovering the new King of Rock 'n' Roll. Jill responded to his warmth, just as Tod had. She smiled broadly and put out her hand for a shake. Elvis took it like a cavalier and gently kissed the back of her hand. Jill blushed; her mother beamed.

"Well, gotta go. Good seeing you again, Mrs. Taylor. Bye, kids. See you, Lootenet." He was obviously in a hurry to do his shopping and get the heck out of there before any teenagers recognized him.

I was struck at the time that he addressed us in the parting order a gentleman would choose, not in the order military protocol would dictate. My wife noticed it too. "Well, for heaven's sake. What a gentleman he is!"

This little anecdote about Elvis is important to me. He got some bad press for a few things, but Elvis Presley had something special that a whole lot of others lacked. He honest-to-God came right from his heart with most people. Someone had given him the values involved, whether it was Gladys, Vernon, Minnie Mae, or one of the other people I have since read about. Elvis had a heart as big as all outdoors. I regret that I never took the opportunity to do what I routinely do with people who are special to me—put my arm around their shoulders and tell them how I feel. But I was much younger then, and overly concerned with the proper distance to be kept between officers and enlisted men. I didn't even put my arm around Ira Jones when we parted for the last time. We just had a long, firm handshake, which conveyed a lot to each of us. In the PX with Elvis Presley, there was that same strong handshake and eye contact. I think it communicated what both of us felt.

*   *   *

As it turned out, we saw Elvis again only a few minutes later. We were leaving the PX to walk the few hundred yards back to our Little Texas apartment, and he was coming out of the provost marshal office, which was next to the PX. He had to walk past us to get to his car.

As Elvis opened the door of his white BMW convertible, Jill said, "Oh, what a pretty car."

"Ya' like it, Jill?"

"Oooh, can I ride in it?"

Elvis looked at Peggy. "Is it okay, Mrs. T.?"

Peggy replied, "We just live down there," pointing to our apartment at the end of the road.

"Sure, we'll be right there." Elvis opened the door for Jill, and she jumped in with a big grin on her face. The engine caught on with that tight, muffled sound of precision power, and the car backed out and headed slowly down the road toward our apartment. Then it turned around, came back to the intersection near the PX, and turned again toward our apartment. This happened two more times before we had pushed Tod's stroller up to our front door. Obviously, Elvis was giving Jill her first joyride.

Elvis parked the car, got out, and walked around to open the door on Jill's side.

"Your servant, Ma'am," Elvis said to Jill, who was beaming.

Jill gave him the most adoring look and put her hand in his. She turned around to me. "Daddy, he's so nice."

Elvis had shown an interest in Jill, had taken her seriously, had been thoughtful to her, and had won her heart in only a few minutes. He kept holding her hand, looking down at her, then at Peggy and me. "You sure have a fine little lady here."

Peggy thanked Elvis and took the kids inside to get ready for dinner. I looked at Elvis and just said, "Thanks a lot. A little thoughtfulness goes a long way in life."

I was standing next to our car and, changing the subject, said, "Well, I've got to go down to the PX gas station and get some parts for this beast."

Elvis looked over our shiny, black 1952 Ford two-door with a "shaved" hood and rear deck, lowered rear, and big dual exhausts. The "beast" was in perfect condition because I worked on it at every opportunity for relaxation.

"Nice. This a '52 or '53? I got a '53 Ford panel truck back home. What you got under the hood, Lootenet?"

"Big Caddy," I replied.

"No kiddin'. I got a big Caddy back home—my favorite car in the world. Can I see?"

"Sure." I walked to the front bumper and popped the hood open.

"Damn, Lootenet, that's big! What's all that stuff on it?"

"Well, it's basically a 1955 Cadillac V-8 that I got out of a junkyard, but I bought an adapter kit for the transmission and had a friend cut and weld new front motor mounts. I also changed the gear ratios in the transmission and adapted a Columbia vacuum-shift, high-speed rear."

"Boy, that's somethin'," said Elvis. "Anything else?"

"Yes, just before we shipped out from New York, I put in an electric fuel pump going to both carburetors."

"That's not a stock Caddy manifold. Doesn't look like mine."

"No," I replied, "that's an Offenhauser dual manifold."

"I'll bet this thing will move," said Elvis.

"Yeah, maybe not quite as fast as your BMW at the top end of the speedometer, but a hell of a lot faster from zero to sixty. This thing can beat anything on the streets from zero to sixty. Well, at least anything I've come up against."

"Nice. Real nice. What you gettin' at the gas station?"

"Well, I hope I'm getting the right kind of points and condenser, but I'm not sure they have what I need. The distributor is a special. I'll just have to go through what they've got and keep matching by inspection. Otherwise, I'll have to write to the States and order. I should have brought a few sets of spares with me, but just didn't have time at Fort Knox."

"When you gonna tune her up?"

"Tomorrow, unless something comes up."

"Want some help?"

"Sure. You want to come over? I'll get the beer."

"Don't drink booze, Lootenet, but I'd like to help out. You'll need two people."

Elvis obviously knew that when you set the distributor point gap, someone had to be in the car turning over the ignition just right so that you could get the tang in the middle of the points aligned with a high point on the distributor cam. That is, unless you had a special tool using a separate ignition switch with wires and clips to hook onto the starter solenoid. I had made one but left it back in the States. And, having tried Peggy's patience more than once by getting her to "click" the starter switch, I knew that I really could use a second person who understood what needed to be done.

"That would be great," I told him. "How about sometime in the afternoon?"

"Good with me, except I got a football game at the house about lunchtime. How about 1400?"

"Great. I'll be right here getting started. Thanks again for being so nice to Jill."

"Pleasure. See you tomorrow."

Elvis drove away, and I drove over to the PX gas station. It took a while, but I found some points and a condenser that would work. I decided to put in some new spark plugs too.

When I got home, I went up to the apartment to play with the kids, help Peggy get dinner ready, and change clothes. I grabbed Jill under one arm and Tod under the other, and we "flew" into bed for some horseplay.

Peggy yelled, "Don't mess up the beds."

We froze, and Jill said, "Isn't he wonderful!"

"Who's wonderful?" I asked as Tod bit my arm.

"Elvis!" This little girl was not gushing over rock star Elvis Presley but over a person who had been attentive and kind to her. She was responding, as he did, in a genuine way.

I thought again about how important it is to go the extra mile with other people. There's a saying, "What goes around comes around." It's true; you'll get back in kind what you give to others.

I have no idea whether Elvis Presley ever thought very much about that, and I don't know how he treated everyone around him before he entered the army. But I *do* know about him at work in the army, and I know how he treated my family. Being nice to people seemed to come naturally to him.

As we were falling asleep that night, Peggy murmured, "What a wonderful day. Elvis Presley was so nice." That was the thing she remembered most about the day. Elvis had made some new fans—and without singing a note.

Elvis called about two o'clock and Peggy took the call. I was already outside the apartment. I had considered going over to Ray Barracks to the Company B maintenance area to use a vehicle ramp, but decided I really didn't need to. Anyway, I would have had to let Elvis know about the change in plans, and I did not have his phone number. Peggy opened our second-floor window and gave me the message: "Bill, Elvis is leaving now." The drive from his house at 14 Göethestrasse was about five minutes. Not many people would call to say they would be five minutes late.

I thought about how lucky I had been to find matching points and condenser for the tune-up. I had already gapped and changed the eight spark plugs and had laid out the necessary tools in front of the car, including an experimental, spring-loaded screwdriver. My father, an electrical engineer, had been given this new tool by an employee. Anyone who has ever fumbled with the distributor screws when putting in new points knows what I'm talking about: you could hardly get your fingers and a screwdriver in position without dropping the screws down into the distributor base and losing the damn things. This new tool "locked" a screw onto a sort of driver and guaranteed that you could get the screw started into the threads. Then you could "click off" the tool and play with the screws and feeler gauge to get the points adjusted properly with a regular screwdriver.

Elvis pulled up a little after two. "Hey, Lootenet, you already started?"

"No, I've just laid things out."

Elvis was in blue jeans and short-sleeved pullover and looked like he had just worked out.

"Have you been out running or something?"

"No, Lootenet, like I said, just a little pickup, touch." He meant touch football. "Good fun. You just gonna change points and condenser?"

"Well, that's for starters. Then I may want to screw around with adjusting the carburetors, depending on how it runs with the new points. By the way, I changed the spark plugs a little while ago."

"I can do the points and condenser," said Elvis.

"Okay. You want a Coke?"

"Sure, thanks."

I had a cold one on the floor of the driver's side—and a cold, local beer too. I opened both, and we took a couple of swigs.

He asked, "Where's the new stuff?"

I handed him the set of points and condenser.

"Use this," I said, and handed him the new screwdriver.

"What is it?" he said, looking at this totally unfamiliar tool. I told him what it was and showed him how to use it.

"Okay! This thing is a great invention. I want one."

"Can't get another one now. It's not in production yet. Someday it will be for sale."

I watched Elvis work, to be sure he really knew what he was doing and wouldn't screw up "my baby." But he went right for it: (1) taking off the two chrome carburetor air cleaners, (2) moving to the distributor at the side of the engine, (3) taking off the side clips on the distributor cap, (4) removing the cap, (5) pulling off the rotor, (6) using a regular screwdriver to loosen the screws 7) using the experimental driver to take out the old and put in the new points and condenser in careful, reverse process. He picked up the feeler gauge I had laid out to measure the point gaps and said, "Okay, Lootenet, give me a shot." I got into the car and turned the key a quick click. "Okay, again." I did. "One more time." I did. "Good. Now one more time."

He adjusted the points, locked down the screws, put the rotor and distributor cap back on, locked in the distributor cap hooks, and asked, "Start it up?"

"Yeah. You clear?" When I saw him move away from the engine compartment, I cranked it over. The engine roared to a start and ran with the rocking, powerhouse motion it was designed for—ready for the accelerator to feed the fuel from the electric fuel pump into the carburetor to produce massive torque.

I shut it down. "Got it right," I said, as I got out of the car.

Elvis looked at me and smiled, then I looked back down at the engine and said, "Just right, I'd say. Got time to take it out?" The autobahn (German expressway) was only a short distance away from Little Texas.

"Sure, let's go."

"You want to drive?" I asked.

"Sure do, Lootenet." Elvis opened the door and got in. "Holy cow, what is this?" he said as he looked at the dashboard.

I explained, pointing out various instruments to him. I had put in a custom dash with mechanical gauges that were much more accurate than the electric gauges that had come with the car. A mechanical tachometer was right in the middle of the dash, tilted left toward the driver's seat for good observation. The tachometer cable ran through the fire wall and looped back to attach to the transmission. The heater controls were under the dash and the radio was in the glove compartment, with a switch that turned the radio on when the compartment door was opened and off when it was closed.

"Who built this?" Elvis asked. He looked surprised when I told him that I had done it myself.

Elvis, as I was discovering, had lusted after, nurtured, and worked on hot rods from about age fourteen on—when he could afford it. To the two of us a perfectly running engine of any sort sounded like Beethoven's Fifth (or "Blue Suede Shoes"?), and the smell of oil and gas was like the smell of a perfect spaghetti sauce to some people.

Elvis turned the key, and the engine kicked over immediately. He backed out slowly, turned down the road past the PX, onto the main road from Bad Nauheim, and drove at about 2,500 rpm toward the autobahn entrance, the *Einfart*. When he was on the autobahn, he asked, "See what it can do?"

"Sure, let it go."

Elvis floored it, and the rear tires screeched and smoked, propelling us forward. The acceleration drove us back against our seats.

"God almighty!" Elvis yelled, smiling like the Cheshire cat and concentrating on the big, broad highway. "This thing moves!"

There was a black BMW sedan ahead of us, moving at maybe 80 mph. I told Elvis how to click the Columbia rear into higher gear. He tried twice, then did it, and we shot past that BMW like it was standing still. I don't remember our rpm's at that point, but Elvis had us at almost 100 mph. He was having a hell of a good time. We could have pushed the Caddy engine more, but I had never driven with Elvis and wasn't 100 percent sure he could handle it. Anyway, the next exit was coming up.

"Want to get off and head back?" I asked.

"Sure." He let off the pedal, started downshifting, and let the beast go into a fast deceleration. He was about to enter the off-ramp and head for home when a black Mercedes with a tan convertible top came up next to us. It was a German guy, maybe a thirty year old, with a damn good-looking blond woman.

Elvis was clocking maybe 40 mph or so at that point—going at a normal speed toward our *Ausfart* (exit). The German guy gunned his Mercedes, and the blond waved bye-bye.

"Whadaya' think, Lootenet?"

"Whatever you think. Yeah, put it down!"

Elvis jammed the accelerator to the mat. The beast didn't burn rubber at that speed, but the acceleration was like dynamite. We shot forward. We caught and passed the Mercedes in an instant. Elvis let off. The Mercedes came up to us. Elvis floored it and got two to three hundred yards ahead of them in an instant. He let off, obviously loving the fact that he could play with them.

The next exit beyond Bad Nauheim was coming up. "Whadaya' think, Lootenet?"

"Let's go home."

Elvis turned on our right turn signal to make sure the Mercedes knew we were cutting over in front of him to get onto the exit. The Mercedes backed off.

Elvis said, "Look at that!"

I looked back at the Mercedes, now passing on our left. The blond was standing up in the passenger seat, waving, and blowing kisses. She had on a tight white sweater.

"Holy shit, look at those things!" exclaimed Elvis. He wasn't looking at the car.

Elvis downshifted, let it back down, eased right, and went down the Ausfart. We had to circle back onto the autobahn to get back to Bad Nauheim. It was getting close to 4:30 P.M. as we again entered the speedway.

As Elvis eased into the Einfart, a BMW sports car—a white convertible just like Elvis's—with two good-looking young girls in it bombed by us. I didn't say a word. Elvis floored it again, with determination and a "Hot damn!"

Here we go again! I watched the tachometer fly through 5,000 rpm and head up fast.

"Would you look at that?" Elvis said.

The girls were waving at us, even the blond doing the driving, as Elvis raced up next to them. The girl driving yelled something in German. Neither one of us understood the words, but the message was definitely "let's go."

Well, we were already going right by the BMW and fast. But Elvis let off the pedal and stayed next to them for a bit. Hair flying in the wind, the girls laughed and smiled. Elvis was smiling, waving, and having a blast. The turnoff was coming up.

"Don't you think we ought to get off here?" I asked Elvis.

"Yes," he agreed reluctantly.

We got down to maybe 2,500 rpm and eased off to the right, still decelerating. Of course, the BMW did the same.

We were now on the road that would eventually pass the Little Texas apartment complex and PX on the way to Bad Nauheim.

"Hey, Lootenet, want to stop at that Gasthaus?"

He pointed to the left at a quaint little Gasthaus on a side street very close to my apartment. In fact, I saw the place every time I looked out our bedroom window. Sometimes we walked to a little bakery next to it to buy Bröchen.

"Sure."

Elvis turned left, slowed down, and parallel parked. Sure enough, the white BMW pulled up right behind us. The girls got out in a hurry and quickly walked up to Elvis, the taller beauty with an excited but somewhat quizzical or disbelieving look on her face.

"Elvis Presley?" she half asked, half gasped.

"Hi," he said with a grin, getting out of the car.

They each grabbed an arm and pressed up against him in wild-eyed ecstacy, carrying on in excited German. "Ooh, vee drink, bitte?"

"What do you think?" he asked me.

"Sure, why not," I replied, thinking, what harm could it do? If I had more than one big beer, I could just walk home. Elvis didn't drink, so he could walk to his BMW and drive right back to his place.

The shorter of the two girls, a brunet, grabbed my arm as we walked across the cobblestone street to the front door of the Gasthaus. There was no one inside except the hausfrau, who smiled and welcomed us in German. I pointed to a table in a corner, and she nodded, saying, *"Ja, bitte."* Elvis and I pulled out chairs for the two girls, and we all sat down. The girls and I ordered beers, and Elvis pointed to a poster advertizing an orange drink.

We tried out the little German we knew, but the girls, who spoke much more English than we did German, carried the conversation. The brunet pressed my arm, "Your name?"

"Bill Taylor. Your name?"

She said, "Heidi."

The way the first few minutes had gone, it appeared that the taller blond had laid claim to Elvis, and Heidi had settled for me. She seemed happy enough about the situation and didn't say a word about the fact that I was wearing a wedding band. What the hell, I thought, this isn't a pickup: these two girls had just lucked into a once in a lifetime, chance meeting with Elvis Presley and his friend.

The blond was twenty, and Heidi nineteen. They worked as secretaries in Frankfurt and had been visiting school friends in the town just beyond Bad Nauheim. During the first few minutes, the girls got Elvis's autograph on the back of several beer coasters—so did the hausfrau after the girls told her who Elvis was.

We ordered a second round of beers. They were good, local brews and pretty strong. We kept working through broken English and German as we talked—mainly about Elvis's life, his songs, his plans for the future, and so on. I was as interested as they were.

Elvis talked about growing up in Tupelo and Memphis. The blond asked about his parents.

"Well, my pa and grandma are livin' with me here. My momma just passed on."

"Oh, so sad," said Heidi.

There was a long pause. Elvis seemed to have lost track of the conversation. I had seen this happen once before in a casual conversation at Grafenwöhr when someone had asked about his parents. Evidently, he was having trouble adjusting to his mother's death. Maybe his mind just turned inward to focus on something sad or happy about his relationship with his mother. I couldn't tell because the expression on his face was totally impassive—no look of pain or joy, no nothing. His eyes were blank and expressionless.

"What is the last movie?" asked the blond.

Elvis snapped back to life.

"*King Creole*, just before I joined the army. But there were three others, too."

"*King Creole*, was it fun? Did you have beautiful girls? Did you kiss any girls in the movie?" asked Heidi.

Elvis smiled again. "It was okay. Too fast. Too much to think about. Yeah, some girls."

"What is your favorite song?" Heidi asked.

"So many hit songs. How many?" asked the blond.

"Well, maybe 'Lonesome Tonight' is my favorite. There have been fifteen or sixteen other pretty big ones."

"Oooh, yes," was the response from the blond, who was staring into Elvis's eyes with rapture.

"My mother and her friends do not understand," said Heidi. "They say your music is bad for us. They do not like it if I listen to your singing because it is full of sex. But I like it very much."

Elvis looked down at his hands, then looked at Heidi with a half-smiling, half-quizzical expression. "We're sorta' different in the States these days from what I see here in Germany. But we're gonna be more like each other in a few years. Life is funny that way. You're learnin' some things from us, and I'm learnin' things here from ya'll. So's my family and friends. A few problems, but it'll all work out okay."

"Jaaa," breathed the blond softly, her elbows on the table, hands folded under her chin. Her expression was angelic but intense. Her elbows were not the only things on the table, and I could see that Elvis had noticed.

Heidi asked about where he lived, and Elvis launched into a long and wistful description of Graceland and what a fun place it was for him, his family, and his friends. He talked about how beautiful Graceland was, about the stables and his love of horses, about swimming, about touch football games with his friends, about how much he liked being alone in his own special room. It was a rambling collection of thoughts, but Graceland began to take shape in my mind as a magnificent place that could have been very peaceful and reclusive, but probably wasn't.

Heidi continued her interrogation: "Do you like German food?"

"Sure do. But some people think I like unusual things."

"Yes?" questioned the blond.

"Well, I like things like bacon sandwiches with lots of mustard, and I like peanut butter a lot."

"Peanut butter?" asked Heidi with a puzzled look.

You should have heard Elvis trying first to describe peanut butter, then what peanuts were and how they were grown, then how they were turned into butter. There was more than a little confusion going on at this point in the conversation. I tried hard not to laugh out loud; it was like watching Elvis try to describe an elephant to a blind person. He really wasn't very good with analogies and looked quite frustrated as he tried to make his A plus B equal C—the C being peanut butter. I'll guarantee you that he did not succeed.

"How long will you be in my land?" asked the blond.

"Oh, another year or so."

"You will go back to singing and films?" she asked.

Elvis paused and looked reflective. "I hope so, if people don't forget me. I'll be away a long time. There are lots of other singers and movie actors out there. They tell me that if you're out of sight, you're out of peoples' minds, or sumthin' like that. While I'm in the army, I'm out of sight to people who used to listen to me."

"Hell, Elvis," I said, "you've got songs and movies playing all over the place in the States. And your fans know what you're doing and must respect that. You've got it made. They'll be all over you the day you get off the plane or ship."

"Ja, ja, sure. But now *we* have you," said the blond with a beautiful, happy grin and her palms held up flat to emphasize the plain certainty of her statement.

"Ja, it is good for us," exclaimed Heidi, looking first at Elvis, then me.

"*Ja ser gut,*" chimed in the hausfrau, obviously not missing a word from her position near the bar.

A crazy idea occurred to me as I watched this: the Germans had lost the war but now they had captured the King of Rock 'n' Roll. I started to chuckle.

"What's so funny, Lootenet?"

"Oh, just had a crazy thought, Mr. PFC Presley."

Then the inevitable question: Did Elvis have a girlfriend back home? More important, did he have a local girlfriend?

The replies, given rather sheepishly, added up to "No, not really."

"Do you like German girls?" the blond asked in a coy way. "And, do you like me?"

"Yeah, sure do," said Elvis with a studied smile, putting his hand on top of hers on the table, and leaving it there as he talked. Then, apparently as an afterthought, he put his other hand on top of Heidi's. He didn't want Heidi to feel left out. Once again, there was Elvis caring about another person's feelings.

The girls talked about their lives for a while. They had been little girls, about my Jill's age, during World War II. Their town had never been bombed, but they remembered being scared by the stories they had heard about the war, about people being killed in the bombings of Frankfurt. They had been afraid of all soldiers, Germans or Americans, back in those days. Tank columns rolling through their town's main street had frightened them. Their parents had always hurried them into the basement of their house whenever the sound of planes or tanks could be heard. Yes, they had been taught in school how bad a man Hitler was, but Germans did not know it in the 1930s. No, their parents had not known about what Hitler did to the Jews.

Heidi, who had been listening intently to Elvis's every word, dropped her hand from the table and onto my lap. Our casual conversation was getting out of control! I looked at my watch, hoping that no one would notice. It was 5:45 P.M. Elvis and I had driven away about 3:30. Peggy would be getting worried. And I was getting worried too! I knew damn well that it was time for me to get out of there. Elvis and the blond were totally focused on a different conversation at that point, still holding hands.

Heidi's hand was starting to explore. Decision time! I leaned over, gave her a soft kiss on the cheek and said, "You are very beautiful and very nice, but I have to go home now." Simultaneously, I put my left hand down on her hand and gently lifted it back on top of the table. Neither Elvis nor the blond seemed to notice. I reached into my trouser pocket, pulled out some deutsche mark bills, slipped them to one side of the table, and said, for *all* to hear, "I live just across the street and that field, and I have to get home for dinner. You all don't need to leave now. I'll see you later."

"Ooh, so soon?" said the blond.

Heidi stood up when I did, gave me a little hug, and said, smiling, "You are very nice, Bill. Maybe we meet again."

"I hope so." Then, looking at Elvis, "I'll just drive the Ford around to the house. Stop in if you want, or I'll see you tomorrow."

Elvis stood up, smiling broadly, shook my hand, then sat back down. "Lotta' fun, Lootenet."

I went over to the hausfrau, who was behind the bar. *"Danke,"* I said, pointing to the money at the table. She saw it, smiled, and said, *"Danke shöen."* I left by the front door. Well, almost. Elvis had the car keys. As I opened the front door again, he was there to hand me the keys.

"I'll stay a little longer. See you, Lootenet."

Back out on the cobblestone street, I could see the lights from the bedroom window in our apartment. I got in and cranked up my baby, more than satisfied with the instant, pulsing growl of the Caddy engine. It took me only a couple of minutes to turn around, cruise back past the PX and into my parking slot. If the trees at the edge of the field just beyond our apartment hadn't been there, I could have thrown a rock halfway to the Gasthaus.

I locked up the car and went upstairs. Jill came running for a hug and kiss.

"Where have you been?" asked Peggy.

"Presley and I stopped at the Gasthaus over there for a drink."

"Oh. How's the car?"

"Runs like a champ."

"I'll bet," said Peggy, who was not exactly a hot-rodder, but who put up with my hobby with more patience than most wives would have.

"We ran the Ford out on the autobahn for a while," I said as I walked into our bedroom and looked out the window. The girls' white BMW was still parked in front of the Gasthaus. I went into the kitchen, gave Peggy a hug and kiss, then walked over to the living room window overlooking our parking space; Elvis's white BMW convertible was still parked there.

I didn't look again for maybe thirty minutes. When I did, both BMWs were gone. I thought, all's well that ends well—I guess.

The next morning, I was up at the usual 4:30 A.M. and into my B Company office around six o'clock. I always liked to "push the papers" early, when no one was around, so that I could spend the rest of the day in total contact with our men.

It was hard to resist seeking out Elvis to find out how the previous evening had ended. But I did resist, and neither he nor I ever brought it up in later conversations. I didn't because, in retrospect, I realized that I shouldn't have said yes when he suggested driving over to the Gasthaus. Probably, he never brought it up for the same reason—or because it was none of my business. In any case, the point was that Elvis had the good common sense not to trade on a bit of overfamiliarity. Our relationship in the next few months always remained very friendly but militarily proper. That was the way we both wanted it.

CHAPTER 7

ELVIS IN THE FIELD—
SPRING TIME

I t was in March 1959 when Elvis and I hit Graf on field maneuvers together again. I had been promoted to B Company commander. This trip would be our last time—and best time—out in the field together. My company would have a field test and I was excited about that. Also, I felt I was really getting to know Elvis Presley as a human being.

We were to meet again one night around our battalion headquarters while the entire battalion was out in the field in a simulated tactical situation. I had received a radio message to report to headquarters for a command and staff meeting. On that lovely spring night my jeep, B6, approached the headquarters area with driving lights out.

"Halt, who goes there?"

It was a security challenge from one of the guards staked out in hidden positions to prevent any of the aggressor force from entering the tent area where battalion headquarters had been set up.

"Lieutenant Taylor, B Company."

The guard gave the challenge words for the night—words contained in the classified SOI (standing operating instructions) which were printed in a little booklet carried in the breast pocket of all officers and NCO leaders in the battalion. Like everyone else, I had memorized the challenge and password for the day, and I gave the prescribed reply.

"Recognized. Okay to pass," said the guard.

As in previous trips to the field, platoons from other battalions or from the division's 83d Recon Squadron had been sent to Graf to serve as aggressors against units being tested. Occasionally, one of the units of our own battalion would be assigned aggressor duty. I had heard that the scout platoon had finally been given the aggressor mission on this field training exercise, rather than serving as a guard unit for the battalion headquarters area. The headquarters guard mission was a job any recon man hated, and it was a gross misuse of scout platoon capabilities. The change in the platoon mission hadn't come by accident. I had fought hard for this change, and I had won.

After the command and staff meeting, at about nine o'clock, I left the headquarters area, taking a different route. My jeep got challenged again, a bit unusual when leaving a secured area. After giving the password again, I decided to dismount and see who was providing security. My eyes had adjusted to night vision after leaving the inside of the lighted headquarters tent and I could see the shape of a jeep parked in the dense brush close to a tree foliated with new spring growth. A soldier about my size emerged from the shadows.

"Who goes there?"

"Lieutenant Taylor!"

"Squires here, Sir. How are you, Sir?"

I asked how things were going, which I probably shouldn't have done, since the guy was from the mortar platoon—the unit that had been given the unpopular headquarters duty in place of the scout platoon.

"We don't like this headquarters duty, Sir, and they say *you* gave it to us a while back."

This guy was serious, and I guess I couldn't blame him. I tried to explain. "Come on, Squires, recon is all about moving, seeing, listening, and reporting. For the mortar platoon the name of the game is getting into position, registering the weapons, being ready to fire, move, and set up again. You know that." He just listened and did not appear to be impressed. I asked where the scout platoon was.

When I found out at the command and staff meeting that the scout platoon was on aggressor duty that night, an idea began to form in my head. My B Company, which had been pulling maintenance all day, would be getting a good night of sleep in a nontactical situation and would be nontactical the next day, waiting for our company test two days later. I decided that I would rather do something else—like aggressor duty. Impulsive? Sure. But with my very competent executive officer in charge of administration and maintenance in a nontactical situation, why not? Life is serious, but whoever said you're not supposed to have fun? If I could find the scout platoon, I planned to have some fun. Let the rest of B Company have a few beers and get a good night's sleep.

Squires told me that they were a few miles away on aggressor duty. I asked where, approximately, he thought they were. He told me. It occurred to me that he might be sending me off on a wild-goose chase to get even, so I decided to double-check. I thanked him and departed in my jeep, then called on the administrative (not tactical) battalion radio frequency and got the coordinates for the scout platoon.

I found the platoon within ten minutes, and the first person I encountered was Elvis Presley with his scout squad pulled off near an intersection of trails. I asked him what was going on. He explained that the platoon was preparing for an operation in a few hours to penetrate a tank company position and take prisoners, including the tank company commander.

I dismounted my jeep, and we shot the breeze for a few

minutes, talking about aggressor duty. Whenever there was an opportunity for aggressor duty, I jumped for it, and that's really what I wanted to do that night.

I checked in with Sergeant Jones and asked him if I could join in the night exercise. If he had even hesitated, I would have quit right there, but he was pleased. "Go on, Sir, glad to have you."

I found Elvis and told him what I wanted to do. He got a devilish look on his face. "Count me in, Lootenet."

I went to my jeep and radioed a call to my B Company executive officer. I told him that I had something to do in an area near battalion headquarters and that he was in charge of the company during cleanup and maintenance operations. He still could reach me on the radio. I had great confidence in my executive officer and thought it would be good for him to take command for a few hours. Of course, that line of thinking was largely a rationalization, an excuse for me to have some *fun*— if my plan worked out.

I walked back over to Elvis's jeep and helped him get ready. We had plenty of time: it was now only 9:30 P.M., and I wanted the people in the tank company to get good and tired before we began our infiltration. I set 2:00 A.M. as the time to begin moving toward the company perimeter. Sergeant Jones had several aggressor teams operating at various locations around that tank company, and he and I coordinated the location where Elvis and I would attempt to break through their night security.

The moon was up by this time and it was so bright that it seemed almost like an overcast day. Elvis and I painted each other's faces with camouflage grease, taped down the excess material on our sleeves and trousers, taped our dog tags so they wouldn't click together, taped over our name tags and rank insignia, and took the plastic blocking out of our fatigue caps. While Elvis was peeling tape off a roll, I noticed that his fingernails were bitten down to the quick, and I wondered why.

While we worked we had time to shoot the bull about things in general. This was one of those rare occasions when we actually had time to discuss anything in depth.

Elvis was the one who started it. "Lootenet, what's goin' on in the world?"

The minute he asked that, two or three other guys nearby overheard and walked over. They all knew damn well that I loved to answer that kind of question.

"Well, guys, things are mixed up right now. The Berlin crisis is not over, and that situation is one we'll all have to watch because our butts could be ordered into combat at any minute." There were serious nods.

"The good news is that despite the Berlin crisis, Vice President Nixon is meeting with Khrushchev in the Soviet Union. I don't know what to make of that, except that it sure as hell has to take the edge off the confrontation over Berlin. That's good news for us, if I've got it right. But, let me tell you that the Soviets are feeling their oats. They've got thermonuclear ICBMs, long-range missiles that can reach the United States, and huge military forces expanding everywhere they can. They're moving well beyond Europe into what people call Third World nations all over the globe—the Middle East, Asia and the Pacific, Africa, Latin America. In my opinion, the Soviets will continue to try to scare the shit out of us in mainland Europe and Asia, but their main moves will be to force or convince people in parts of the world that are poor and backward to become communists and work with the USSR against American national security interests. They're moving into certain countries where they can establish naval bases, for example, in Southeast Asia. And they are building naval combat ships fast.

"When we get back to Friedberg, I'll get out some world maps for you and show you what worries me. The United States is a seagoing nation. We have to get resources for our industry—oil, special metals for airplanes, and a lot more—from nations in the Middle East and Africa. If the Soviet navy could close off some of the narrow sea-lanes our trading ships have to pass through, they could strangle our industry. We've got some strategic problems in front of us. The question is whether the American public understands all this."

Elvis muttered, "Shit, I don't think Americans even want to know about this stuff. A lot of people I know back home think I'm out of my mind doin' what I'm doin'."

One of the others said, "You got that right."

I shifted the subject. "There's another thing. You know President Eisenhower's two terms are about up. There's the new guy, Senator Jack Kennedy, running for the presidency. This guy is a Democrat with some new ideas about the world. He's a lot younger than Ike. He's making noises about recognizing the new threats to our security. He's sounding tough, but he doesn't have a hell of a lot of experience on foreign policy issues. On the other hand, he served in the navy in World War II as a PT boat commander."

My driver got animated. "Doesn't mean he knows anything about bein' a soldier on the ground, like this stuff we're doin' tonight."

It was dark, and they probably couldn't see me smile.

Elvis said, "Well, he can sound tough if he wants to, but I'm tellin' you that most people I know don't want any more Korean War kind of stuff. I mean goin' around the world and gettin' killed because some politician wants to show how tough he is."

I've often thought about what Elvis and his friends said that night. They may have sounded naive, but they had it right. These guys reflected the mood of America's youth, who were on a different wavelength than America's elected officials, business leaders, and their parents and teachers. Elvis and his friends sensed that America was heading in wrong directions, that older people were not listening to their concerns, that priorities were screwed up. A "youth revolution" was occurring, and Elvis and his friends understood it better than I did.

This formerly poor, not-too-well schooled kid from Tupelo knew what most of us did not know. Simply put, a whole lot of young people thought the older generation was all screwed up. These young people were *not* going to accept what they thought was bullshit.

The other two guys finally started to talk about something else and ambled away. But Elvis stayed. We had opened up to each other on any number of personal matters, and Elvis seemed to feel free to talk about various aspects of his life. So I asked him a question that had been on my mind. I had passed Elvis's home on 14 Göethestrasse a few times, and I had seen the almost constant crowds waiting outside the white picket fence to get an autograph, photo, or at least a glimpse of Elvis. I had often wondered what it was like to live in a fishbowl. So I asked, "Does it bother you to be the center of attention all the time?"

He was sitting down on the fender with one leg propped up on a big rock next to the jeep.

"Well, it depends. I feel good about a crowd in front of me when I'm on. If I'm pumped up about a good show and the people like it, I'm on a high along with 'em. That's when it's good bein' around crowds. It gets old when they're hangin' around home. Sometimes I don't even go out the front door. I jump the fence and run outta' there."

I asked about the people I heard were living with him.

"I'm lucky to have Daddy, Dodger, and some of my best friends here. It can get lonely sometimes."

I could understand that. Even with all my buddies around when I was in OCS, I was lonely as hell without my wife and baby. It's never how many people are around you, it's who they are.

I asked him where he had grown up and what his father did for a living. Elvis shifted around on the jeep fender.

"Well, Lootenet, life growin' up wasn't easy. We didn't have a pot to piss in. Daddy was a sharecropper until we moved to

Memphis, then he got work wherever he could get it—deliverin' milk, workin' in factories, or doin' whatever he could to make money. When I got old enough, I helped out by mowin' lawns." He paused, then said, "People looked down on us then."

Elvis asked me about my early years. I told him that I had been lucky; my dad was an engineer and had been able to send me to a fine private school. But I told him that my father had always worked long hours, and he made sure that I worked for spending money by cutting lawns, cleaning out bilges on the boats of the Delaware River (the smell made me vomit every time I went down the ladder), or working at a gas station. My father wanted me to understand that nobody gets something for nothing in life.

Elvis said softly, and reflectively, "You better believe it. You *better* believe it."

He asked what I wanted out of life, and I told him that I really did not know for sure. I said that I had taken a regular army commission thinking about the army as a profession, but my wife wanted me to get out and go back to college. I told him that I thought I could be as good an army officer as anyone but worried that my lack of a college education would hold me back.

Elvis said, "Well, I know that you take college courses at night back at Friedberg."

"Yes, but it's going to take me forever." I must have sounded a bit dejected.

Elvis waxed philosophical. "You'll do it, Lootenet. You gotta believe in yourself. Just know who you are."

Hell, I was the one who had studied the world's great philosophers, and here was this young guy from Memphis telling me how to approach life. I smiled. "Yes, you're right, my friend. By the way, you sound like my father."

He laughed out loud—too loud for our own night security—then I did too, trying to muffle the sound.

"I guess your life is pretty well laid out for you, Elvis," I said, thinking that I had seldom called him by his first name. He didn't seem to notice.

"Well, maybe so, but I'm not sure what I really want. You better believe I'll have plenty of help decidin'. Movies or records? How much time on the road? Whether or when to get married? Have kids? Who my real friends are?" He threw out a string of quick questions with no answers, holding both palms up in a questioning gesture.

He slapped his knees softly. "Hell, I got plenty of time to decide when I get out." He yawned and stretched.

I really liked this guy. No ego, no bragging—just a normal, nice guy. Sergeant Jones had told me that Elvis periodically bought gifts for everyone in the platoon for no apparent reason. And Sgt. Billy Wilson told me once that Elvis had given a hundred dollars to one of the privates in the platoon whose parents had been killed in a car crash, leaving several orphaned children. Most of the scout platoon guys were from very poor families. Elvis just seemed to feel good about helping other people. He must already have received megabucks from his records and movies, but he sure didn't flaunt his wealth around any of us. He did drive that BMW sports car, but he didn't make a big deal out of it as some people would have—he drove it because he appreciated high-performance cars.

Elvis asked, "When are we gonna take off, Lootenet?"

I reminded him that two o'clock was the time we had set, and he held up his wrist to check the time. It was about eleven.

He said, "I'm kinda' hungry, but all I got left is hamburger patties and crackers. I gave the good stuff to my buddy."

When you got a box of C rations, which we ate while out on maneuvers, you never knew what would be inside. Sometimes you got lucky and sometimes you didn't. An unlucky box would contain, for example, a can of hamburger patties or a can of tinned, scrambled eggs (god-awful even when heated), a can of crackers, a can of tinned jam or peanut butter, a round chocolate pattie, and an aluminum packet with a small pack of cigarettes, a pack of matches, another small piece of candy, and a napkin, plus a tiny hand can opener called a P-38. (The P-38 was so useful that many soldiers attached them to the dog tag chains worn around their necks. I don't know where the no-menclature "P-38" came from, but everyone who served in the army of the 1950s knows what this two-inch-long thing is and what it could do.) A lucky box of C rations had a can of beans and franks, or ham and lima beans, and crackers. Best of all, a can of fruit (pears, peaches, or mixed fruit in a thick sweet syrup), plus the aluminum-covered pack of cigarettes, and the rest of the stuff were in a lucky box. C rations were always a surprise, like opening Christmas presents.

I told Elvis that he was in luck. My B Company driver and I had four individual meal packs with us. They all contained beans and franks and fresh fruit.

"Hot damn. Let's heat 'em, okay?"

I walked over to my jeep, which my driver was starting up regularly to keep the battery charged. I had to keep my com-mand jeep radios turned on in case my B Company exec or the battalion commander needed to get in touch with me, and the radios could drain the battery pretty fast. Elvis followed me and greeted Mac. The jeep was running, so we knew we could get a hot meal fast.

Mac raised the hood, and I handed three boxes of rations to Elvis. He opened one and grinned broadly as he lifted out a can of beans and franks. He put the can on the hot exhaust manifold of the engine. Mac put on two more cans. We'd have hot chow in five to eight minutes. Elvis was really hungry, however, and decided not to wait for the beans and franks. He pulled out his P-38 and opened a can of pears. He used the little can opener like a pro, holding the can down with one hand and working the sharp edge of the opener up and down with the other. He opened the can only halfway, bent the lid open, drank the syrup, then let the pears slide into his mouth one at a time. Then he spotted the can of peanut butter. "Hot damn!" He quickly opened the peanut butter and a can of crackers and devoured it all. Elvis did enjoy his food—even C rations.

"Not bad, Mac, thanks," he said.

Elvis put down the empty peanut butter can and reached over the top of the engine to feel the beans and franks can. He missed and touched the exhaust manifold.

"Oh shit," he exclaimed. As he jumped back, he slammed the back of his burned hand on the side of the jeep hood. Again, "Oh shit," as he put his hand in his crotch. "Son of a bitch!" He grimaced at Mac and me.

I couldn't help grinning. "Jesus, Presley, here you are a walking wounded, and we haven't even started our operation."

I walked over and looked at his hand. There wasn't enough light to see his hand clearly, despite the bright moonlight. I could barely make out a thin dark line on the back of his right hand and the beginning of some minor bleeding.

I took off my canvas web belt and removed the poncho that was folded and tied on the back of the belt. I opened the poncho.

"Here, sit down and let's get under this." I put the poncho over our heads so I could use my flashlight to examine his hand. We were "tactical" out on maneuvers and couldn't take the chance that someone might see the light. Under the poncho I turned on my flashlight. The plastic "dimmer filter" didn't permit enough light, so I unscrewed the holder and removed it. I looked first at his burned fingers. There were no telltale white patches, so I figured the burn was not a problem. I grabbed his wrist gently to take a look at the back of his hand— only a little scratch there from a jagged edge on the jeep hood. It wasn't at all serious, but I decided to treat it anyway. I reached down to my cartridge belt on the ground, took my medical packet off the web belt, opened the snap, and pulled out the aluminum packet containing a bandage and a pack of sulfa powder.

"Lootenet, I don't need that," Elvis protested.

"Hell, that's your playing hand. No chances." I tore open the powder package and sprinkled some on the back of his hand. Then I opened the bandage packet, pulled out a penknife, cut gauze away from the bandage, and wrapped Elvis's hand. I split the ends of the gauze so it could be tied.

"There, no infections. Let's eat."

"Lordy, Lootenet," Elvis muttered.

Mac had already taken the cans off the exhaust manifold before they got too hot to handle. Elvis and I stood a minute with eyes closed to get our night vision back after having our eyes exposed to the flashlight. After a minute, Mac handed us the cans, which he had just opened, and two spoons, from his mess kit and mine.

"I'm not hungry now," said Mac. "Had some other stuff a little while ago."

Elvis and I ate all three cans of beans and franks, biting off pieces of tinned crackers as we chewed. It was pretty good when you were really hungry.

Mac had taken the shovel off the side of his jeep and was digging a shallow hole a few meters away. He collected the empty cans and other trash, put them into the hole, and covered them up with dirt. He tramped it down with his boots. All soldiers on maneuvers knew the rule was that you had to bury your trash, not leave it littering the German countryside.

I looked down at the luminous dial of my government-issue watch with an olive-drab, nylon strap. (Each company had a few of these watches for "key personnel"—the officers and a few NCOs. I always wondered why the army logistics planners thought enlisted men didn't need to be able to tell time. No doubt, watches were more expensive back in those days.) The time was a little after midnight.

"We've got a couple of hours until we kick off," I told Elvis. "Then it will take us about an hour and a half of walking and crawling to get to that tank company's defense perimeter. So let's talk out a plan."

I didn't say *my* plan because, whenever there was time, I liked to talk through a plan that my men could help develop. This made it *our* plan and served as a powerful motivator. And, quite often, I picked up a tactical idea that had not occurred to me.

So, we began to put together our plan. I started talking, and Elvis cut in pretty often with a "Well, howsabout" or a "Don't ya' think we outta'."

After talking through what we wanted to get done—capture the tank company commander—we got back under my poncho with a flashlight. I pulled out two maps. One was a 1:50,000 coverage of the general area. The other was a 1:2,500 coverage of the precise area where we were located. I had brought these with me in an olive-drab, fiber-composition tube with a canvas carrying strap. This map tube had been given to me by my Headquarters Company commander, Capt. Jack Cochran, when I took over the recon platoon in 1956. It was from his days in the Korean War and was no longer authorized for issue, but I found it handy. Cochran, along with Ira Jones, taught me that a recon man needed to know map reading "down to a gnat's ass" and should always have the pertinent maps in hand before beginning any operation. I had gotten a complete set of maps for the Grafenwöhr training area a couple of years earlier, and they sure had helped me—as they would now.

Elvis and I located ourselves and the tank company we planned to infiltrate on the two maps. We both had compasses with luminous dials strapped onto our cartridge belts. We checked out our compasses and slipped them into pockets. We would not be wearing cartridge belts or any extraneous equipment on this exercise. There were too many things hooked onto our cartridge belts—including a canteen, first-aid packet, bayonet, and poncho—that could catch on branches and weeds and make noise.

Elvis looked at the 1:2,500 map *very* carefully. "Well, we don't have too far to walk—maybe a mile or so?" That was interesting to me. I recalled what he had said to Lt. Ron Spurlock on the way to pistol shooting.

He was right, but it didn't surprise me. Anyone trained in that scout platoon had had hundreds of hours of map-reading classes. A novice cannot operate from a 1:2,500 map, where one inch equals twenty-five hundred meters, and contour lines show elevations at roughly 20-meter intervals. That takes special training.

Elvis pointed to a certain location on the map. "We got to climb a steep place here, right under where those tanks are sure gonna be."

"Yes," I agreed, "we can go there the tough way—straight up—or go east around here where it's not so steep."

Elvis grunted, "Uh-huh. And the easy way is where they'll expect us to come. Why don't we go the hard way?"

"That's up some tough rocks. How's your hand?"

He looked at me and smiled. "Nuthin' to it, and I'll put some grease paint over the bandage so they can't see it." The bandage was a pinkish color and would be visible against the dark color of mud and foliage.

I was impressed by Elvis's comments. This was the kind of thought process and behavior that would eventually get Elvis his sergeant's stripes. He really used his head when it came to doing his job. Even though he hated maneuvers, and like most of the men, would rather be doing something else, when he was there, he got into it and paid close attention. He had been made a scout team leader, and I could tell that he thought and cared about the soldiers in his squad. For example, he had given the best of the C rations to one of his men. This is the way a decent leader always thinks. The people under his supervision come first. A good army leader never eats before his men, and he makes sure that they get the best and enough if there is any shortage of food. In combat, you can't afford to lose leaders, but a leader in ground combat units who doesn't share the risks isn't much of a leader.

Elvis and I worked out a plan that seemed to make sense. I had done this kind of planning scores of times over the five years I had already been in the army. This was Presley's first time. He was clearly getting a charge out of it and was eagerly anticipating what was to come. I turned off my flashlight, and we got out from under the poncho again, closing our eyes to readjust to what we thought was a moonlit night. But in the half hour or so that we had been under the poncho, clouds had blotted out the moon. It was pitch black, and there was a wind coming up that smelled like rain.

"I think we're gonna get wet, Lootenet."

"Yeah, but at least it won't be cold," I said, referring to the winter field maneuvers in Graf only a month or two before. In fact, rain would work to our advantage in this aggressor exercise. And, as described earlier in the book, our mission was an unqualified success. We penetrated the security and captured the command post. Also, we enjoyed working together. It was a night both of us would remember.

A day or so later, we were back in the Graf central area—where the motor pool, barracks, and hot showers were—to rest a couple of days before our next maneuver out in the field. It was a chance to clean up and relax. Now, my mind was on my own B Company command test. I felt *ready!*

We trained hard at Graf. The old saying is that "soldiers fight the way they train," and we knew we had to be ready to fight anytime. But soldiers are people, and even in a major training area there had to be some time for rest and recuperation from the long, exhausting drills out in the field.

It was on an unusually sunny, clear, and crisp Sunday afternoon that Elvis and a couple of the scout platoon guys stopped by the officers' quarters looking for me. I was sitting outside on a tree stump in front of a table made of a board laid across two five-gallon gas cans, cleaning my .45-caliber pistol with bore cleaner and oil.

Elvis saluted nonchalantly. "Lootenet, you gonna clean the bluin' right off that thing."

He was right; the Colt .45 automatic I had been issued was old as hell, and the dark, dull finish was wearing off right down to the steel. You didn't want the damn thing to shine—that might give away your position to the enemy. But I didn't care how my weapon looked as long as it worked.

Elvis had a beat-up football in his hand and started throwing it up and down with a twirl. "Lootenet, it's Sunday—time to relax. You got a couple of officers who wanna play touch ball? B Company doesn't go into the test until tomorrow."

How in hell did he know?

I was about finished cleaning the pistol and was planning on doing some running for exercise anyway. I smiled broadly. "Thanks for asking. How badly do you want to be beaten and by how many of us?"

"Well, Lootenet, do you think you can find two more officers young enough to run?" Elvis was having fun ragging me. He knew I had a sense of humor.

I thought it was great that he had come to me to ask for a game. "Well, let me find out. Wait a minute."

The rest of the guys were inside reading, studying map reading, writing letters home, or whatever. We had some damn good college athletes among our lieutenants, and when I asked two of them whether they wanted to play touch football with Elvis Presley, they were ready to go in no time flat.

"Okay, Presley, let's go. I hope you guys are up to this." Hell, this would be a cakewalk—or so I thought. I had played football from fourth to twelfth grade and could outrun most of the guys in the battalion. And I knew my other two guys were good—*real* college football players. I figured we could have fun and win at the same time.

"Ya' know, Lootenet, we ain't bad at two-hand touch." There was that funny crooked smile—the same smile Elvis had on his face the night we captured the captain's headquarters while on aggressor duty. Elvis Presley had lots of different smiles, and I thought I understood what was behind each one. I had gotten to know the casual "everything is alright" smile. It was a relaxed, slow smile, with his teeth showing just a bit and his eyes closed a little as his cheeks went up. It was a smile that meant that he was content and that you were his friend. Sometimes I saw a big, broad grin when something hit him as amusing. This crooked smile was different: it said, "I know something you don't know."

I stored my .45 in our makeshift arms room and was ready to go. The six of us had already introduced ourselves, so we started walking down the dirt road to an open field.

Elvis was unusually talkative. He got that way when something important was about to happen. He got "psyched up," as we say nowadays. I could almost feel his adrenaline flowing. That didn't bother me because I was getting a bit "pumped up" too. I loved competition, thrived on it.

We got to the open field, bordered by a road and two lines of cinder-block buildings. Elvis said, "Here you go, Lootenet," and tossed the ball to me.

"Go on out," I said and waved him to my right, toward the trees.

Elvis took off at a run and half turned about twenty-five yards out, yelling, "Hit me. Hit me." I looped the ball out, leading him, and he gathered it in easily. He stopped, turned, and waved me off to my left. I ran out, ready to take his pass. I was running at a forty-five-degree angle, getting closer to him as I went. He fired the ball, and I caught it on the go, feeling the force of a damn good rifle pass. He had a good arm.

One of the privates yelled, "Here you go, Sir." And I fired one to him at close range. He caught the pass in his gut in midair and kept running like a rabbit. That guy could catch, and he was a fast mover. He stopped, pointed to one of my guys, a tall Texan over six feet four with hands maybe twice the size of mine, and waved him over to the left. "Tex" snared the pass in his big hands, stopped, waved one of Elvis's guys out to the right—at pretty short distance, maybe fifteen yards— and fired a pass so damn hard that when Elvis's guy caught it in the chest, it knocked him down like a rock. We seemed to be pretty evenly matched.

"Okay, time to play?" yelled Elvis over to me. "Two-hand touch?"

"Sure, let's go," I said, pulling a metal deutsche mark out of my pocket. We all knew the German equivalents of heads or tails. I said, "Call it."

Elvis called, "Buzzard side" and won. "We receive, Sirs," said Elvis.

The field between the road and buildings wasn't all that big, maybe sixty to seventy yards long by about thirty yards wide. But that was plenty of room since there were only six of us in the game. We weren't going to do any fancy sprint running either, because we were all wearing heavy, leather combat boots.

We took off our fatigue uniform shirts and laid them out to mark goal lines, then I yelled, "Here we go!"

Touch football rules vary. We could have passed, simulating a kickoff, but it was more fun to kick, so I put the ball down for Tex, and he booted it high into the air. The shortest guy on Elvis's team caught it behind the line of fatigue shirts at his end of the field and took off fast down the center, then darted off to his right. He faked me out, and Tex was not fast enough to catch him. My other guy touched him on the arm, but with only one hand, so off the runner went like a scared rabbit for a touchdown.

I turned around to see Elvis standing at midfield with a shit-eating grin on his face. It changed immediately to a quizzical expression when he saw me looking at him. "Well, just beginners' luck I guess, Lootenet." Who cared—now it was our turn!

One of Elvis's guys held and the other kicked right to Tex, who was the slowest of we three officers. The rabbit on Elvis's team came blazing down the field heading straight for Tex; Elvis was not far behind him. Tex shouted, "Hey Bill, here!" and lateraled the ball to me where I was running on his left and a step behind him. I caught the lateral and had a pretty clear field because Rabbit and Elvis could not stop their momentum toward Tex. Elvis's third guy was out of position, and I raced over the jackets at their end of the field. One touchdown apiece. We went back to our respective ends of the field.

Our third officer, Mike, kicked off as I held. The ball wasn't kicked very well. It rifled off to the side along the ground, well short of their goal line. Elvis caught it on the bounce and cut toward center field, but Mike was there to tag him with two hands. Now, it was their first down.

They huddled and came out with Elvis as quarterback. Rabbit was their line runner, and their third guy centered the ball from the crouch position, facing Tex. The ball snapped back to Elvis after a long count. I blocked Rabbit for a couple of seconds, and Tex knocked their guy playing center flat on his ass. I ran for Elvis, who dropped back to his right, cocked his arm, and threw a long, looping pass over all our heads to their third guy, who had outrun Mike. It was a perfect pass just beyond our field jackets, and it was their second touchdown. We were behind by one score.

They kicked off right down the middle, and I received. All three of them started to converge on me, and I cut left. Rabbit was on me in an instant. His two hands "touched" me on both lower legs, dropping me like a sack, just as if I had been tackled. Wham! Down I went on my left shoulder, and the ball squirted loose from my grip. Guess who picked up the loose ball and ran for a touchdown? You got it—Elvis. He trotted back toward us, saying, "What's the score? Who's winnin'?" as if he didn't know. He couldn't resist ragging us.

I just smiled. "It ain't over yet, Presley."

We received again, and Mike had a pretty good run back, roughly all the way to their twenty-five-yard line. We huddled and made up a passing play to begin on a short count of two. Mike was to run fast to the center, then cut left, where I was to hit him with a fast pass close to their goal line. Tex would center, fall back, and block for me. As the huddle broke, Tex muttered, "Kick ass."

Tex got down in the centering position with Elvis opposite him. "Set, one, two," and Tex snapped the ball back to me. I dropped back, saw Mike run out to the left with Rabbit a step or two behind him, and overthrew the damn ball. I uttered a couple of words you wouldn't say in church and looked over to the line of scrimmage where Tex and Elvis were both on the ground. Elvis was in the fetal position and obviously in pain.

I ran over to him. "What's wrong? What hurts?"

"Aw shit, right in the balls. Just wait a minute."

There was nothing to do but wait until the pain passed.

"I'll be okay, Lootenet. Just give me a couple of minutes."

Tex had gotten up and was looking down, slowly kicking the grass with his boots. I wondered what had happened, but there was no use saying anything to Tex.

I knelt down by Elvis. "You sure you're okay?"

"Not a problem, I'm comin' around." He slowly got to his knees, then stood up all the way. "Okay, let's play," he said.

There was enough doubt in my mind about Tex's attitude to lead me to say "We've had enough. You guys are too good. You're a bunch of ringers." We had gotten up a sweat and had some fun, so why push our luck with a big guy whose temperament was unknown? I put my arm around Rabbit's shoulders and said I knew where we could get a cold beer.

We ambled back up the dirt road toward the cinder-block buildings that served as our barracks. It wasn't proper to ask enlisted men into the officers' barracks, so I said, "Meet you in that grove of trees behind the tank park." We all knew where it was. Everybody said okay except Tex. I was relieved to see him go, and, based on the expressions on everyone's faces, they were too.

I got a few of the beers and Cokes that the officers had chipped in to buy for our quarters and stuffed them into a small army backpack. I grabbed the pack and headed for the grove of trees. The guys were there, sitting on the ground or leaning against trees, and shooting the breeze.

"How are your balls?" I asked Elvis.

"How's your ego, Lootenet?" he replied with a chuckle.

"Not funny, Presley. You play too much touch football."

"Oh, now and then."

"How about you?" I asked Rabbit.

"Sir, we play together all the time, every chance we get, over at Elvis's place or wherever."

I passed out the bottles of beer and the Coke for Elvis. We didn't have cans in those days. Each guy took off his dog-tag chain and ripped off the bottle top with his P-38. We took a swig or so without saying a word—just enjoying the brew and the company. It was maybe five o'clock, an hour before evening mess. The sun was going down and there was a slight nip in the air, but we had our fatigue jackets back on. We all knew that we had training exercises the next morning and would have to be up early—four o'clock.

Elvis broke the relaxed silence. "We gotta get up early. What's the battalion gonna do?"

He was grinning again!

I had been briefed on the exercise on Saturday afternoon and knew exactly what the battalion was doing on Monday morning.

"You been briefed?" I asked.

"Sorta'. That the scout platoon is up at 0400 and we get a mission."

"What time are you moving out?" I asked.

"Not supposed to say, but I hope we don't have to lay out any road guides."

Elvis looked much too quizzical. "Lootenet, every swingin' dick in this battalion knows how to get to Hophenoe church. Why do we ever need to put out road guides?"

"My friend, don't ever assume anything. Let me tell you my definition of an assumption. It's the mother of a screwup. Don't ever assume that because you know something, everyone else does. In my few years in the army I have seen so many mistakes happen when the old guys in a unit assume that the new guys in the unit know things. First, tank commanders— the guys who are in the turret watching the road and giving directions to the driver—change a lot. Second, when a tank loader, who sits inside the tank and doesn't see outside, is promoted to tank commander, he would never have seen the routes around our training area. Third, you know that driving in darkness while trying to read a map is not easy. Reading a small-scale map is something that most people can't do. There are lots of ways to get lost while driving at night. *You* don't get lost because Sergeant Jones reads maps while you drive," I needled.

Elvis sat there scratching his crotch. "Yeah, okay, but I wonder exactly what we are gonna *do*."

Mike chimed in. "We're doing whatever battalion tells us to do."

Rabbit asked with a half smile, "What the hell are we doin' this for anyway?"

Elvis joined Rabbit's sentiment. "Yeah, Lootenet, just why are we?"

When my soldiers asked me a question, I tried to answer to the best of my ability. In this instance, my explanation to Elvis and Rabbit would bore you to death, but shorthand for what I said was something like:

- We're serving in our nation's army.
- Our people count on us to deter war or fight it well if deterrence fails.
- The Soviet Union is a big threat to American interests all around the world, not only to our homes in the United States, but to our friends and allies here in Europe too.
- We want to deter the USSR from attacking.
- The best way to prevent them from attacking is to make them know that we are so well trained that we will beat the hell out of them if they attack.
- We are good enough to do this if we train the way we'll fight and make it a habit.
- You and I are training to do this.
- All five of us sitting here are better than any five people of our ranks the Soviets can put together.

"What's deternz?" one of them asked.

I tried to take all questions seriously, even those that might have seemed obvious to me. "The word is *deterrence*, spelled d-e-t-e-r-r-e-n-c-e. Comes from the verb *to deter*. It means you keep someone from doing something you don't want him to do."

Both Elvis and Rabbit got confused looks on their faces.

"Let me give you an example. There's a big guy in your neighborhood who doesn't like you and has told people that he's going to kick your ass the next time he sees you. You know he's big enough to do it too. You want to *deter* him from trying to start a fight with you. How can you do it?"

"Yeah?" said Elvis, sitting up straight. He gave me a knowing smile—he and I had been in a conversation like this at Graf only a few months before.

"Well, there are a few things you can do. First, you could get the word out to him that you know karate and that his big frame would just present a big kicking bag for you. The guy may believe it and leave you alone. Or he may call your bluff and try to beat the hell out of you. So, it's obviously better to actually know karate and have a black belt to prove it."

Elvis was watching Rabbit, who was listening intently. Elvis just cut into the conversation and started talking.

"It's just like what we're doin' in our relations with the Soviets. We don't want that big ass army of theirs attackin' us. So we have a hell of a lot of units in Germany, includin' us. We tell the Soviets that our tanks and other equipment are so good, and that we're so damn well trained, we could kick their ass if they were ever dumb enough to attack us. But the Soviets have spies around, and we had better really be well trained. If not, they'll know it and may not be deterred from attackin' us."

There were positive nods all around. I was impressed as hell that Elvis remembered the logic of what I had told him and even more impressed that he was actually sitting there teaching others—and loving it. He was smiling like the Cheshire cat.

I said, "Wait a minute, let me finish.

"There's another way to deter," I told them. "Think back to the big guy in your neighborhood who wants to beat you up.

You send out the word that you've got lots of friends in your gang who will help you fight him if he ever tries to lay a hand on you and that your friends are good fighters. That may deter him from coming after you. But you'd better be seen around the neighborhood with your friends, and they better have reputations for being good fighters."

"You mean like the other battalions of our division?" asked Elvis.

"Not exactly. I mean like our NATO allies."

"What does NATO mean?" asked the third soldier.

"NATO—North Atlantic Treaty Organization. It's our gang of sixteen other nations who have agreed that, if the Soviets attack any one of us, we'll all fight together against the attack. NATO includes European nations such as France, England, Germany, and Norway. Even Canada is a member. We have a NATO headquarters in Brussels, Belgium, and that headquarters, commanded by a U.S. general, is our overall boss who commands us all in our mission to deter the Soviets from attacking. All the other nations train their units just like we train. And Elvis is right—the Soviets have spies all over the place to see whether those other NATO units really are well trained."

"Yeah, okay," a couple of the guys mumbled, nodding that they understood.

Elvis jumped in again. "There's a lot more to deterrence than that. Even if I know karate and even if I travel in a gang, the Soviets have to know that I'll actually use my karate and that my gang really will fight if they attack. Do I really have the will, the guts to fight? Will my gang really hold together in a fight, or will some of them run?"

"Yeah?" questioned Rabbit.

"You tell him, Lootenet," said Elvis.

I was more impressed every minute with what Private First Class Presley was saying.

"Well, all the nations in NATO are democracies. Do the people of all our sixteen nations—our presidents or prime ministers, our congresses or parliaments, and our publics—

have the will to fight if war breaks out against one or more of us? How about if lots of our soldiers are killed and wounded in war—will our people continue to stand behind us?"

"How about the Korean War?" asked Elvis.

"Right," chimed in Mike. "Explain that one."

"Good question. That's been a big debate. We didn't lose the Korean War, but some say we didn't win it either because we stopped short of defeating the North Koreans and Chinese."

"So?" asked Rabbit.

"Well, after about thirty thousand Americans had been killed, and more than a hundred thousand wounded, Americans couldn't see the point of continuing their support for the war, especially because no one in our government could define victory for them. It was our first 'limited war,' and that's not the kind of war Americans understood and would support."

"So, what was different about World War II, for example?" asked Elvis.

"First of all, America didn't want to fight the war in Europe for several years, until Japan attacked us at Pearl Harbor. Then President Roosevelt called for complete and total victory. It was democracy versus dictatorship. Americans knew what the objective was: surrender by the Axis powers—Italy, Germany, and Japan. The closer we got to Rome, Berlin, and Tokyo, the closer we got to victory. With an objective they understood and with progress toward objectives they read about in newspapers, heard about on radio, or saw in movie house newsreels, Americans were willing to send their sons to die for the right cause and to sacrifice with rationing of gasoline, oil, and many kinds of food at home."

"Yeah, they sound like different kinds of wars alright," said Elvis.

Something important had just happened. I knew after this discussion that Elvis Presley really had an intellect. He and I had discussed the concept of deterrence only once. That guy had heard and digested every word I had said. I wondered whether he had ever taken the college SAT exams. Then I thought, it really doesn't matter. He didn't need to go to college. Elvis Presley was already having a major impact on our generation.

Elvis was looking up at the sky. "Lootenet," he said, "you'd make a good schoolteacher. You make plain sense. That's why we come to see you. You know what I mean?"

Yes, I knew. And that comment meant more to me than any rave review from my superiors.

I looked at my watch. It was 5:45 P.M. These guys had to get back for chow formation, and I had to prepare for a meeting with my exec and platoon leaders in the morning. The big company test was coming and we had an inkling that the scout platoon just *might* be the aggressor!

"You guys ready to go?" We all shuffled our butts up.

"Let me have the bottles," I said, and they all put their empties in my canvas pack. We walked off toward the main barracks area.

Elvis and his two buddies dropped off at the enlisted men's quarters. We threw each other casual, friendly salutes, and I continued walking toward the BEQ (bachelor enlisted quarters) where Ira Jones was staying. I decided to pay my respects to the Old Pro. A few NCOs were standing outside the door, and I asked one of them whether Jones was there. Sergeant John Callender saluted, then shouted, "Hey, Sergeant Jones. Lieutenant Wild Bill wants to see ya'."

"Be right out," came the long, low Arkansas drawl that I had come to know and enjoy over our three years together.

Out ambled Jones without "cover" (no cap on) and an unbuttoned fatigue shirt hanging out. "Good ta' see ya', Sir."

"You guys ready for the company?" I asked.

"Toujours prêt," he replied in southern-drawl French and with a big grin. "Always Ready" was the motto of his previous reconnaissance squadron.

We shot the breeze for a few minutes about our families, when our "rotation dates" (time for reassignment to the United States) were coming up, and other such matters. I already had my orders to be assigned to command a company of the 67th Armor at Fort Hood, Texas. Jones was due to get his orders in a few days.

All of a sudden, we heard shouting and laughter from the enlisted barracks.

"Probably Presley, Sir. When it comes to horseplay, Presley ain't got no equal."

Sure enough, the wooden screen door flew open with a bang and out charged two stark-naked soldiers—Elvis chasing Rabbit with a pail full of water. They looked ridiculous, with wet hair and dicks swinging in the breeze.

"Son of a bitch!" shrieked Rabbit as Elvis hit him in the chest with the water, which I assumed was ice-cold. Then Elvis dropped the pail, laughed raucously, and bounded back into the barracks with Rabbit in hot pursuit.

Jones chuckled, "Well, morale's up as high as ever, I see."

"Sergeant Jones, morale is always high wherever you are."

"Soupy, soupy, soupy," the bugle recording sounded throughout the area.

"Time for chow," I said.

"See you out in the boonies, Sir."

At 9:00 A.M. I headed over to my meeting with my executive officer and platoon leaders to go over our two-day tank company attack exercise. I knew pretty well what the drill had to be: (1) an early-morning road march in the dark to an assembly area, (2) movement to contact, (3) crossing an LD in attack formation against whichever of the four or five big hills in the Graf training area that would be occupied by an aggressor, (4) defeat the aggressor, who would be firing blanks and exploding big firecrackers to simulate combat, (5) consolidate our position and resupply fast, preparing for a counterattack, (6) establish a night defense perimeter, (7) conduct a daylight attack on a second objective, (8) repeat consolidation of another objective, (9) tactical daylight road march back to the Graf wash racks for cleanup and stand down. This roughly nineteen hours of tactical exercises would be graded by umpires. The aggressors could harass and attack us at any time, at the places they thought we would be most vulnerable.

After five years of military education and one hell of a lot of field training, I didn't plan on my company being vulnerable to anybody—not even to Elvis's scout platoon, with an old pro like Ira Jones and a bunch of guys who knew me so well. I had thought really hard about this exercise, especially in light of Elvis's needling. First, I had to think through what the aggressor would expect me to do, then I would do the opposite, or at least vary my usual method of operations. That meant first and foremost that I had to confuse and disorient the aggressor "control." I had to be totally unpredictable. But I had to let my exec and platoon leaders know what I was thinking and why, if I expected them to be prepared for different tactics.

First of all, I decided that when we started our early-morning road march, at some juncture we would take a different route to the assembly area from the one that we were assigned (and that Jones, Callender, Wilson, and Elvis definitely would find out about), maybe even by moving off the road and going cross-country. Of course, I would have to give headquarters a good reason why, such as my suspicion that the aggressor had mined the road or a bridge. Second, I would request permission to switch to an alternate radio frequency so that the aggressor couldn't monitor my communications. Third, I would find a reason to request switching my company assembly area position with the mythical tank company on my left or right, meaning also that my company's axis of attack would put us hundreds of meters away from where the aggressor would expect us. Fourth, I was determined not to stop on the objective but to request that I be permitted to press the attack against an aggressor in retreat, requesting air strikes and artillery to cover my flanks if I got them exposed by outrunning other companies. Fifth, in my night defensive position, I would put LPs so far out on low ground that aggressor patrols (including Elvis, who would think back to our night patrol experiences together) wouldn't expect to find them there and might run into them by accident. Sixth, I would have a "ready reaction" squad prepared to respond immediately to any firm LP report on aggressors in his area and overpower the suckers! That squad would come from my company maintenance section—assuming, of course, that one or more of our tanks wasn't broken down or stuck in the mud. The former was somewhat unpredictable. The latter was a function of the platoon leaders selecting the terrain they took their tanks over, and I planned on talking with them about that *very* carefully. Seventh, I would not permit the platoon leaders to "let down" on the return road march to the main Graf barracks area but would stay on the radio with them, reminding them that the exercise wasn't over until we got a mile or so away from the wash racks. It kept creeping back into my mind that Elvis Presley would have a lot of latitude from Ira Jones and would just love to catch me off guard.

At my meeting I laid out my map of the Graf training area on the hood of B6. "Okay, listen up. Tomorrow morning we start a graded company exercise. I want to talk about that in general. All but one of you have been through this a few times. You guys are good, you know the company SOPs, but what you don't know is that we're not going to do many standard things during this test. Let me tell you why and why you have to be flexible and imaginative as hell. I also need to tell you that if you breathe a word of what we're going to talk about now, we could fail. I have talked with you a lot about 'the fog of war.' We're going to create a hell of a lot of fog for the aggressor."

I had spent hundreds of hours as B Company exec talking the officers and NCOs through military strategy as well as tank company tactics. I had read military history—the works of Jomini *(Summary of the Art of War)*, Clausewitz *(On War)*, Sun Tsu *(Art of War)*—and I thought hard and often about what I read, trying to thoroughly understand the concepts. The great military strategists taught you to get into your opponent's mind, disrupt his ability to observe correctly, screw up his mind so that he makes bad decisions, avoid doing anything he expects, and keep him off balance. All you should care about is seizing key terrain, killing his people, and saving yours. Now, once again, I had a chance to put the theory into practice.

I continued the briefing. "I will be giving simulated battalion orders that will look very familiar to most of you when I brief you in front of the umpires who will grade us. But be prepared for me to change those orders at a moment's notice, and be prepared to react immediately."

The guys nodded their heads in the affirmative, one of them commenting, "This is going to be fun."

"Now one more thing. We're not going to go SOP on our night security. I think that the scout platoon may be the aggressor. They have been itching since last winter at Graf to get at us. Those guys know the way I do things, so I'm not going to have us do things Sergeant Jones, Callender, Wilson, Elvis Presley, and the rest expect. You guys watch me, and when you have a good idea of how to keep those guys off guard, lay it on me fast."

I explained the costs, risks, and high-potential payoff of what I was planning, adding that the ready reaction squad plan would be called off if we lost any of our tanks. I asked the men to check our tanks for any automotive problems.

"Okay, I expect our operations order late this afternoon. Use the day as you see fit. I'll brief you on the OPORD after chow tonight. After you brief your people, put 'em to bed. I'm sure we'll be up very early. Again, don't talk to anyone outside our company about any of this. The scout platoon would do anything to get intel on our plans."

Early the next morning I had my tank company moving on a road march. We headed out toward the Hophenoe church area to be in an assembly area by 4:00 A.M. to prepare for further movement to cross an attack LD at BMNT (beginning of morning nautical twilight), which was to be at 5:45 A.M.

I was in my tank behind the first platoon. We were moving at a very slow pace, maybe fifteen miles per hour, with all lights out and our 90mm gun barrels pointed forward. There was a half-moon, which gave us just enough visibility. After almost an hour on the main road, we were coming up on a dry dirt trail that led directly to the designated assembly area. This trail would cut off a couple of miles of travel onthe road—of course, we were supposed to stay on the road. I got on the radio. "Champion, this is Champion Six, over."

"This is One-Six, over." "This is Two-Six, over." "This is Three-Six, over." "This is Five, over." All platoon leaders and the exec had replied.

"This is Six. One-Six, you'll see a trail coming up to your right front in about five hundred yards. Take it directly to our first destination. All Champion to follow."

All units acknowledged the order.

The next thing I heard was the Control Six umpire.

"Champion Six, this is Control Six, over." Control Six was a senior major.

"This is Champion Six, over."

"This is Control Six. You've taken a wrong turn, over."

"This is Champion Six. Negative, have selected alternative route, over."

"This is Control Six. You can't do that, over."

"This is Champion Six. I already have, out."

That would really hack off the major, but I knew that our battalion CO would back up my initiative—if my plan worked.

Ten minutes later, we approached the assembly area. We were about twenty minutes early.

One of my units called in.

"Champion Six, this is One-Six. I just saw a light in the assembly area, probably a cigarette lighter, over."

Hot damn. Someone in the aggressor platoon had violated night discipline. It wouldn't be Elvis. He seldom smoked, and he knew better anyway.

"This is Six. Assembly area is now attack objective. One-Six, deploy to left flank. Move on line in battle formation. Champion Two-Six, deploy on line to right of One-Six. Champion Three-Six, deploy to right of Two-Six. All load blanks, simulate HE [high-explosive rounds]. Check in when moving on line. Wait for my command to fire."

The assembly area was densely wooded with broad, dry fields to the right and left.

I told my tank driver to pull off the trail to the left, to let the second and third platoons pass us as they maneuvered. I dropped back behind the second platoon, which was in the center of our company line.

We were now about four hundred yards away from the tree line. I had been in these deep woods on maneuvers the year before, and I knew that whoever was in there couldn't drive away from us through the woods. They would have to exit to the left or right—directly in front of my attacking tanks.

"Champion, this is Six. Open fire."

All hell broke loose as fifteen tanks moving on line started firing blanks at the woods. I could see the orange glow out of the gun barrels as each blank was fired, and in the moonlight could make out the large puffs of smoke. We would have to stop firing before we got too close to the dense vegetation, because even a blank could start a fire.

It was time for me to check in with control.

"Control Six, this is Champion Six, over."

"This is Control Six, over."

"This is Champion Six. Engaging suspected aggressor in woods, over."

"This is Control Six, roger. Out." Boy, did that major sound irritated.

When my tanks on line were about seventy-five yards from the edge of the woods, I pushed the microphone button on my chest set. "Champion Two-Six, stop about ten yards from the woods. Champion One-Six and Three-Six, swing left and right to encircle woods, stop ten yards short. All cease fire, over."

Within a few minutes all tanks stopped and sat waiting with engines idling.

A jeep drove out of the woods, then another, then a whole bunch of them using the main trail past my tank. Some were machine-gun jeeps. They were "surrendering."

"Driver, stop engine," I said, then got out of my tank hatch and dismounted over the front slope of my tank. As a jeep came by I saw a front bumper marking. It was a scout platoon, but from the 83d Recon Squadron of our division. They, not our own scout platoon, had been assigned aggressor duty against us! Not Ira Jones, not John Callender, not Elvis Presley—none of the hungry pros. No wonder the lack of night discipline that tipped us off!

What we had just done was to trap and blow away most of the aggressor force. They had not expected us to arrive at the assembly area that early and had not yet dispersed to positions around the woods from which they obviously had planned to harass us. No, this sure wasn't my old platoon.

As I climbed back up into the turret, I vowed that I definitely would not tell Ira Jones—and especially not Elvis Presley— that I had worried during the whole B Company operation about what tricks they had up their sleeves. They would laugh their asses off. No, I would keep this one to myself and hope that no one in B Company would think to mention it to anyone in the scout platoon.

The rest of the operation went as well as it began. We seized the main objective, repelled an aggressor counterattack, resupplied, set up our night security perimeter, and captured two aggressor patrols that tried to penetrate. The men of B Company were on a roll.

The next day, when we were back in the barracks area at Graf and had cleaned up, I threw a company party. We made a special toast to the sergeant in our platoon who had first spotted that cigarette lighter in the assembly area. We later found out that the few vehicles of the 83d Recon Squadron scout platoon that we hadn't destroyed in the assembly area had been out on the main road, waiting to screw up our road march. But, of course, we didn't go that way.

B Company received the highest score ever awarded by our Combat Command to a tank company for its annual test. My response to Elvis's challenge during the winter exercises at Graf had paid off!

The battalion started packing up a few days later to put the tanks on trains and to road march our wheeled vehicles back to Friedberg.

The word got around pretty fast about what had happened. A couple of soldiers flagged down B6 the day before we left Graf. One of them was Elvis. He saluted, and I returned it.

"Lootenet, I heard you're the luckiest guy in the world."

"Private Presley, there was no luck involved. B Company doesn't screw around."

"That's not what I mean, Lootenet. You're lucky that *we* weren't assigned as the aggressor, because you never would have gotten away with all that stuff."

To tell the truth, I *was* glad that Ira Jones's crew had not been assigned as aggressors. They would have had at least one scout squad out on the main road before that tank trail and might have guessed what I was doing. And they would never have been caught flat-footed in the assembly area. No one of them would ever have lit a cigarette in the dark out in the open during a tactical exercise. But I wasn't going to admit it.

"Well, maybe you're right, Presley, but then maybe you're wrong!"

CHAPTER 8

HOUND DOG DEPARTS

After returning from the March field maneuvers, I spent the last few days of the month turning over my B Company command to another officer. I was reassigned as the 32d Tank Battalion assistant S3 for a few days while preparing to leave Germany to go to a training unit, the 1st Medium Tank Battalion, 67th Armor, at Fort Hood, Texas—right next to the unit where Elvis had taken his AIT (advanced individual training) before he came to Germany. The thought of returning to the good old U.S.A. after three years away was pretty exciting. But there was also that thought of leaving so many good army friends at Ray Barracks in Friedberg and German friends in Bad Nauheim. Most of all, I knew that I would miss Jack Cochran, Ira Jones, Elvis Presley, and the rest of the old recon platoon gang. Leaving a good unit is always a tough thing for a military professional—and for others in his unit.

There was to be one more get-together with the old platoon before we left. One of the scout platoon sergeants called me at home to tell me that the platoon was holding a party to pay tribute to Ira Jones, who, like me, would leave in April for reassignment. He asked whether Peggy and I could attend, saying it would be nice to see us before we went home. The party was to be held at a secluded Gasthaus outside Bad Nauheim, on the road west toward Usingen. He said that wives, girlfriends, and "lots of other girls" were invited.

Peggy did not like the kind of "hard partying" that went on in army small units, but she knew this was important to me, so she agreed to go.

On the following Saturday night, I picked up our baby-sitter in Bad Nauheim, then we drove our Ford to find the Gasthaus. The place was quite a few miles away, and I was glad that Peggy, who didn't drink, could drive home because I intended to have more than a few of those great local beers. She didn't like driving the beast because it really was a handful, but I knew she would never let me drive if I had been drinking.

The Gasthaus was located at the end of a long tree-lined country road. It was a big place with a cobblestone drive leading into it. A five-ton truck, a bus, and lots of German and American cars were parked in a big cobblestone parking lot out front. When we walked in, there was a small German band playing, and the place was already hopping—lots of laughter, plenty of beer on the tables, good cooking smells coming from the kitchen, a haze of cigarette smoke. Sergeant Jones, sitting with his wife, Elizabeth, saw us come in and walked over to greet us. We hung up our coats, and he led us over to his table.

Everyone was in civilian clothes as were we. None of the guys wore ties, and the women were mostly in sweaters and skirts. There were a lot of girls in their late teens or early twenties. And no one could have helped noticing that they were all beauties

I said to Jones, "Good grief! This looks like a combined Miss America–Miss Germany pageant." He told me that Elvis had arranged dates for almost all the guys, and he had provided a gift for everyone in the room. So he had. At my place was a small box containing a man's leather wallet, and for Peggy a lady's wallet. Both had "EP" stamped in the leather.

All the guys were from the scout platoon. Lieutenant Ed Hart had already left Germany, and Ira Jones was in command. I was the only officer there. I told Jones that it was nice to be with everyone again before leaving and thanked him for including me.

"Hell, Sir, this party is for you as much as for me."

It wasn't, but it was nice of Jones to say so.

Sergeant Billy Wilson stopped by the table, making a typical comment: "C'mon Wild Bill, we're trying to get you outta' Germany so you'll leave us alone."

He stood there wobbling a bit and raised his beer glass (obviously not the first one that day). "You're gonna be alright," he told me. "Jones and Hodges taught you pretty good." And he laughed loudly.

The hausfrau had put a beer by my place. I raised it and said quietly to those at our table: "Our thanks to you professionals for everything you have done for us all these years, and especially for your loyalty and friendship. To the best recon platoon sergeant and his wife in the world!" We raised our glasses and drank that toast with gusto.

The German band soon stopped playing. Records were now playing rock 'n' roll, and the guys and girls were getting with it. They were really having a ball.

It wasn't hard to spot where Elvis was sitting—and, of course, he had a gorgeous girl at his side. There was a constant grouping near his table, where guys and girls would go to talk when they weren't dancing. Early on Elvis gave the mandatory autographs, but eventually the pieces of paper, record album covers, and photos stopped flowing, and he could just sit and talk. We hadn't been there very long before he came over to our table to greet us.

I had seldom seen him in civilian clothes. He was wearing a striped sport jacket, black or dark blue on gray, a blue shirt with the collar turned up, and dark baggy slacks. He had a dark handkerchief in the jacket breast pocket. He looked good.

"Hi, Lootenet, Mrs. Taylor. How're the kids? You're gonna leave us. Well, I'll be right behind ya'—in about ten months.

Take care of little Jill, she's gonna be a beauty. I wanna see her when she grows up." And so on, to Peggy's great delight.

"Lootenet, can you come talk a minute?"

"Sure." I excused myself and followed Elvis out a side door. We stopped under a big tree.

"Just wanted to talk a minute, Lootenet." He pulled out a cigarillo. "Got a light?" I lit his cigarillo, then my cigarette.

"Thanks for the wallet. Peggy liked hers too."

"Pleasure, Sir. I wanted a minute before we get Sergeant Jones up front. I can't believe that you two are both leavin'. You two have been very important to me. Swear to God, if you hadn't been around, my days would've been a lot different. I really appreciate the time you took when I wanted to talk. I—"

I cut him short. "Look, Elvis, let me tell you—"

"No, Lootenet, just let me finish. I want you to know that you've meant a lot to me. You never laid any bullshit on me or any of us. You really care about the guys. And all of us thank you for it. You're goin' places. That's really all I wanted to say."

He said this with the greatest sincerity, and I was deeply moved. "That's the most important thing you could have said to me. I'll tell Peggy."

He nodded his head, and we both turned to walk back into the party. Elvis walked with me to the side of our table, looked closely at Peggy, and said, "Mrs. T, you're one short of a tank crew." Civilians wouldn't know that a tank crew is four, but a military wife like Peggy did.

"Well, we'll work on it," she said with a grin.

"See y'all later," Elvis said. Then to Sgt. Billy Wilson, who was still standing unsteadily by our table, "Don't get lost on the way home, recon man."

They both laughed.

Elvis looked like he was having fun at the party. He seemed to get around to talk with just about everybody. I don't think he danced, at least not when I was watching. He sat with a cigarillo hanging out of his mouth (it didn't seem to be lit), and he laughed a lot. He was in no way showing off—just being the normal, fun-filled guy that he was.

At one point in the evening, Peggy tapped me on the arm. "Look at Elvis Presley. He is a real gentleman. See how he's getting around to people? I think that he's very different from what most people back home think."

"Most people back home" meant our ultraconservative, privileged friends, many of whom were snobs. I was grateful that I had had the opportunity to meet other people, just plain people, who contribute to society in different but important ways. Military service is a leveling experience.

It was starting to get late in the evening, and the Gasthaus was really rocking. I had danced with each of the wives at our table at least once, when they played something I could dance to. I really wasn't into rock 'n' roll in those days. I liked some of the music well enough but had been pretty well insulated from American trends in popular music since 1954 when I enlisted. I had heard a few Elvis songs and liked the ballads, such as "Falling in Love With You," but could not quite figure out what was appealing about "Blue Suede Shoes" or "Hound Dog." (When I got back to the States, however, I got caught up by the rhythm of rock, made the fairly natural transition from dancing jitterbug to dancing rock, and found myself in the world of the King of Rock 'n' Roll. Believe it or not, so did Peggy. As for Jill and Tod the answer is obvious.)

At about 10:30 P.M., Ira Jones uncoiled his big frame—somewhat shakily—walked to the bandstand, got up on a chair (I thought he was going to fall off), and yelled for everyone to pipe down. He helped draw numbers for prizes and, when they had been handed out, he called out, "Okay, give me your attention." He paused for a few seconds while everyone quit talking—well, almost everyone. Jones looked over to one of the room's corners, pointed toward some pretty loud people, and said, "Hey, ladies and gentlemen over there, I'm talkin' to you too." Someone blew a whistle. Silence prevailed.

Jones announced that Elvis was going to sing. There was a loud round of applause, whistling, and yelling. The guys and girls went wild. Although Elvis played a little in the barracks once in a while, just for fun, he simply did not perform in public, and no one would have expected it. But he got up and walked over to the piano, grabbing Jones by the arm as he went, and seated Jones next to him on the bench. Elvis played and sang several of his great ones, including "Heartbreak Hotel." Then he produced a guitar to sing "All Shook Up," among other pieces. I thought the Gasthaus would explode. Everyone, especially the girls, went crazy. The waitresses, the hausfrau, the maintenance men, and the dishwashers all came out to watch. No one got up to dance, they just listened to the songs, then cheered as if their hometown football team had pulled the biggest upset in the world. They were ecstatic! Near the end, Elivs looked over at my table.

"Lootenet, this next one is dedicated to you. This is for old times, *Sir*. This is for you, 'scuse me—Wild Bill."

Everyone looked over at our table. The guys started clapping and yelling, "Wild Bill, Wild Bill." I figured that I ought to stand up, so I did, not knowing what Elvis had up his sleeve. A few introductory chords shot out, and then it came as only Elvis Presley could do it: "You ain't nothin' but a hound dog . . ."

First, everybody broke out in wild laughter, then they applauded, and then they listened in absolute rapture. Me too. Elvis really got with it! There was wild applause as he ended. He waved to me with a broad smile, stepped over to the piano next to Ira Jones, turned around, waved to everybody, and walked toward our table.

I really wanted to go out on the dance floor and hug the guy. But it flashed through my mind that this was Ira Jones's party and that the best thing for me to do was get out of the limelight. I simply shook Elvis's hand and thanked him. "That was damn thoughtful of you. It was just great."

He grinned like a kid. "You and I know each other, Lootenet. I won't forget you."

"And I won't ever forget you either, Elvis Presley. You're a damn good man—and a damn good soldier."

I turned away from him. I could feel tears coming on.

I went to Ira and Elizabeth Jones and shook their hands— hard—holding their forearms with my left hand. "You are great people. Thanks for everything."

I turned to Peggy, saw tears in her eyes, and knew that we should leave. We did, never looking back.

That was it. I went my way, and Elvis Presley went his.

EPILOGUE

As you can see, I hold a high opinion of Elvis Presley and have been disappointed in accounts that dwell on the problems of his personal life and ignore the positive aspects, such as how well he performed his assigned army duties in Germany and the selflessness I saw him display in so many situations involving the feelings of others around him.

I simply cannot forget the fact that Elvis chose to serve in a combat unit. If others want to argue that he did so because his agent, Colonel Tom Parker, thought it would be good for public relations' purposes, that's their opinion. But I don't believe it. Aside from the fact that our battalion could have gone to war with the Soviets at any time, there are real risks every single training day in a combat unit. I have seen a tank loader's head smashed by a 90mm main gun recoil, hands mutilated or cut off by engine maintenance accidents, an eye put out by blank ammo fired in someone's face, a soldier's body crushed by a tank rolling over it, a leg smashed behind a jeep with a stuck accelerator pedal, horrible burns from fuel accidents—I could go on.

America's superstar did not have to take those risks. Elvis could have gotten out of the 32d Tank Battalion anytime, if he decided not to put up with the bullshit and risk that comes with serving in a combat unit—but he didn't. Or Elvis could have pulled "an Eddie Fisher" in the Army Special Services. He could have spent most of his two years in comfort, traveling around the world to entertain the troops by "rockin' and rollin'"—but he didn't.

I don't know what Elvis said about his army service to Vernon, Minnie Mae, or the "Memphis Mafia" back at 14 Göethestrasse. I also don't care. What I do care about, and what others from the old 32d Tank Battalion—especially now-retired Col. Ed Hart, and retired 1st Sgt. Ira Jones—care a great deal about, is how Elvis Presley did his assigned job and how he related to others in his unit. He pulled his weight. He used his head and did his job well. He was one of us. He cared about us. And he got back the respect and friendship he gave everyone else. In several instances I saw sparks of leadership in Elvis that made me think he could have induced men to follow him into combat, just as his music caused millions of young people to follow him.

Compare Elvis to another national hero, Peter Dawkins. Pete graduated at the top of his West Point class of 1959. He stood first in his class. He was the army football team captain and winner of the Heisman Trophy. He had been selected as a Rhodes Scholar and was on his way to Oxford, England, to study politics, philosophy, and economics for two years. But there was a war in Vietnam.

There is no doubt in my mind, or in the mind of anyone else who knows the army, that Pete could have avoided duty in Vietnam had he wanted to. He didn't, and it surely never crossed his mind. He knew he had to go to Vietnam in the service of our nation, risking a brilliant future and possibly his life. Pete put himself on the line in war, just as Elvis put himself in danger in a combat unit in Germany.

Pete Dawkins loved his country; so did Elvis Presley. Pete trained hard; so did Elvis. Pete took care of his comrades; so did Elvis. Pete was honest; so was Elvis. Pete was a superstar; so was Elvis. Pete was too good a person to let his ego inflate; so was Elvis.

Throughout Elvis's tour of duty people put pressure on him to perform. He didn't. Pete Dawkins had similar pressure put on him for all his army career; he was once asked, for example, to leave his battalion command in Korea to serve as a master of ceremonies for a major convention. He had to fend off hundreds of such requests over the years. Each one was a tough decision. They were for Elvis in the army too.

Why, after his army service, Elvis Presley let personal problems accumulate to the point that they affected his behavior, led to mood swings, and led him to drugs I simply do not know. I wish I did. I wish I could have helped him before he got on that slippery slope to disaster.

Could any of us from the 32d Tank Battalion have helped? I think that the answer is no. Ira Jones tried to get back in touch with Elvis, but the circumstances simply were not right, and the relationship grew distant, then nonexistent. I did nothing more than write a letter to Elvis in late 1961 after I had left Fort Hood, Texas, for duty as a captain with the 10th Cavalry Squadron, the recon unit of the 7th Infantry Division in South Korea.

I remember clearly the day I wrote that letter. It was a Sunday. I had been out early, running with the men of my unit. I had played ping-pong most of the afternoon with Korean officers from a nearby unit. I had sucked down a lot of beer before dinner. The squadron officers had a feast that evening in the Quonset hut that served as our officers' club. A few of us had gone hunting near the Demilitarized Zone, and pheasant was the main dish that night.

By nine o'clock I was back in my room in the cinder-block BOQ (bachelor officer quarters). I had just finished a letter to Peggy and the kids and was thinking about the fact that I would not see them for an entire year, thinking about missing so much of my children's growing up, and wondering how many more times in my army career I would have to be away for so long.

With nothing more to do, having already gone through the routine Elvis had known all too well—spit shining my boots and shoes, shining all my brass, hanging out my freshly starched fatigue uniform—and having thought through my training challenges for the week, my mind reflected back over almost eight years of military service. Almost half of that service had been with the 32d Tank Battalion.

That week I had read a story in the *Stars and Stripes*, the military newspaper printed for servicemen worldwide, about Elvis's rock 'n' roll performances. There was a reference to his alleged drug problem, the first such reference I had seen. I thought about all the times we had spent together—our first meeting, the incident with the German girls at Ray Barracks, the long training exercises at Graf, the afternoon working on the Ford and talking with the German girls, the discussions outside our apartment in Little Texas and next to the pile of manure outside the Gasthaus at Graf, the party where he dedicated a "Hound Dog" rendition to me—and much more.

I ought to write him, I thought. Then it occurred to me that I didn't even know his exact address. My letter would be buried in a bag holding thousands of other fan letters. Whoever sorted his mail probably wouldn't even give it to him, and even if he got it, he wouldn't have time to reply. Writing to him seemed like a waste of time. Result of all the negatives? I decided to write anyway, and managed to get my thoughts down on paper before I dozed off.

"Hey, Lootenet, how ya' been? I heard they're gonna send you to school, then to go teach at West Point. How about that!" There was that Elvis smile.

That wasn't the first dream I ever had that involved Elvis, nor was it the last. Dreams are odd things; you never know why some person or event out of the past creeps in. But, for me, the people usually are characters who, for better or for worse, had an important impact on my life. In those seven months we were thrown together in Germany, a relationship developed between Elvis and me that meant a great deal to both of us. As Elvis said, we *knew* each other.

Elvis Presley was a young soldier of character, a draftee with professionalism, a selfless team player, a man of self-reflection tempered by wit, and—oh yeah—he was also the King of Rock 'n' Roll. I'll never forget him.